STAYING PUT!

The Art of Anchoring

superb, the food satisfying. "Are you sure you have enough scope out?" my wife asked as we turned in. "Sure," I said casually. Three hours later, I felt a slight bump and heard wind thrumming in the rigging. To my horror, we had dragged into the shallows and were firmly aground in a rising onshore breeze. When we pulled on the anchor, it came straight home. It took three hours of backbreaking work to pull ourselves off. Only when we tied several lines together and secured them to a lamp post on a nearby pier were we able to haul her off with two sheet winches and the windlass. Thankfully, we anchored in deeper water. At dawn, the wind came in from the north at 40 knots and we were weatherbound for three days. I think the gods were smiling at my carelessness that night. Ever since then, I have taken anchoring pretty seriously.

Nothing is worse for one's ego than having anchoring problems. Over the years, I have had more than my share of them—usually in front of a fascinated, and sometimes amused, audience. Indeed, one of the truisms of cruising is that it is far easier to make a passage than to stay in one place. Of all the skills you need, none is more important than the art of anchoring. None is surrounded with more arcane jargon and (often) pseudoscience. Yet good anchoring practice is among the most satisfying of all seamanship skills. Some of my most vivid cruising memories are of anchorages and anchoring, of sitting in the cockpit with friends enjoying a sunset or watching fish rise in the quiet of a summer's evening.

I remember anchoring far inside the Florida Keys in a shallow draft 34-footer, lying in 3 feet of water, the hectic world of Miami and the Keys almost on another planet, the only sound the gentle ripple of wavelets against the plywood hull. Then there's the satisfaction of setting the anchor in deep, of lying quietly in a 35-knot wind, the boat swinging in the shifting wind, the anchor rode flexing in the gusts, of knowing you're going to stay put. Of course, there are the dramas, too, the moments when you anchor and anchor again and nothing goes right, when your neighbors drag down on you in the small hours and life becomes a chaotic symphony of wet chain and muddy foredecks. In truth, however, such dramas are far and few between, provided you obey a few elementary rules and take the trouble to gain experience of anchors and anchoring. Anyone can become an anchoring afficiando, provided one's prepared to learn the hard way, by doing it oneself.

This book is about seamanship and good judgement, about anchoring as an *art*, not a science. I believe that safe anchoring is a matter of seamanlike preparation, careful routine, and good, old-fashioned observation and common sense. While such factors enter into the equation, this is not a treatise heavy on anchor weights, catenaries, and all the other technical esoterica that appear at regular intervals in the pages of yachting journals. *Staying Put* looks at the basics and tries to strip away much of the irrelevant mumbo-jumbo surrounding anchors and anchoring. It's a book designed to be read and then applied, a snort, as British humorist P.G. Wodehouse once called it "between the solid orgies," orgies of solid, practical experience. If we help you enjoy your anchoring and to stay put even in very rough conditions, then our job is done.

Why such a mystique about anchoring? Much of it comes from the days of sail, and the time, not too long ago, when cruising yachts had unreliable engines. Our predecessors sailed with monumentally heavy ground tackle, which they handled with consummate skill. They had to: their anchors were much less efficient for their weight. They also used their ground tackle to move their boats across harbors and to accomplish all sorts of other tasks for which we just turn a key today. I vividly remember helping warp a 17-ton, deep draft 43-footer with a long Victorian bowsprit through the Dutch canals in my youth.

The blisters from hours of hauling and towing were with me for days. It was backbreaking work, but the maneuvers we performed with spring lines, blocks, and tackles were miracles in the hands of an ex-naval officer who had learnt his sailing in full-rigged ships. Sadly, such seamanship standards have deteriorated in these days of the reliable diesel. More's the pity. Our congested anchorages cry out for good seamanship.

SOME BASIC PHILOSOPHY

I think that anchoring becomes much easier if you approach it with a coherent philosophy at the back of your mind. My ex-naval mentor was a harsh taskmaster, who had learned his seamanship in a brutal school using technology little changed over many centuries. His philosophy was simple and to the point, and as relevant today as when he learned it in the early years of this century:

• Careful preparation is the secret of successful anchoring.
• Well-established routines make all the difference.
• Common sense and careful observation are essential.

I once saw a marvelous demonstration of the first two principles in St. Lucia. A black-hulled gaff-rigged cutter sailed into Anse des Pitons that evening. The anchorage was crowded, but there were still a few spaces along the beach. The husband and wife crew hove-to close offshore. We watched them start the engine, lower sail, range chain on deck, ease the anchor to the waterline. The dinghy was brought alongside, and a long warp was led from the stern to the boat. Then the skipper went slow ahead. He rounded offshore while his wife stood ready at the windlass. "Drop," we heard. The anchor splashed over the bow. The yacht coursed slowly astern. As she eased to a stop, the skipper hopped in the dinghy and rowed the stern line ashore. Almost before the beach boys knew it, he had tied the line to a palm tree. His wife hauled it in, and they were secured stern-to close inshore. The whole operation was so perfectly executed that we were tempted to applaud.

This couple had made all preparations and were ready for any eventuality. They also had a familiar routine for everything, a routine that freed them to worry about congestion, crosswinds, and other last-minute variables. Both husband and wife knew exactly what each should do, and when. They had practiced everything time and time again.

You can learn preparations and routines from a book, but old-fashioned common sense and acute observation can come only from hard-won experience. I will never forget sailing down the north coast of Santa Cruz Island, California, on a windy spring day with an elderly friend in his 35-footer. It was blowing merry hell from the west out of a clear sky. We were practically surfing, the wind gusting over 50 knots. "Let's anchor in Fry's Harbor," I yelled against the wind. The waters of the anchorage seemed calm compared with the turbulent whitecaps offshore. "No way," said the skipper. "Look at the kelp! It's blowing out of the water. Fry's is untenable when the seaweed's dancing." We ended up in Channel Islands Harbor 30 miles away after a very bumpy sail. Years later, I happened to be in Fry's when the wind blew 50 knots. We had to leave in a hurry. The kelp was dancing and a steep swell ran into the anchorage. My friend's acute observation was accurate.

Let's make an immediate distinction between common sense and fine-tuned observations. The difference is elementary, but often obscured in a mass of cautionary tales and technical admonitions. Common sense is using your eyes and other peoples' experience to make decisions. For example, you enter a sheltered cover and find that two other yachts have anchored under a cliff on the north side. They are close together, when, to the casual onlooker, they could have set their anchors on each side of the anchorage. Common sense dictates that you ask why they are so close together. Unless they are close friends, there is probably a good reason, like, for instance, the dark shadow of a submerged rock that appears straight ahead as you ease your way into the south side of the bay.

Observation is an art that can take years to cultivate, and can really be classified under that magical term "experience." Sometimes it is called "local knowledge," words guaranteed to terrorize the innocent neophyte. You think immediately of crusty old salts leaning against a convenient rail, talking wisely about westerlies, fog, and ebb tides. Or you meet someone in the yacht club bar who smiles mysteriously when you ask about the counter-current that appears to set against the prevailing winds close inshore. Both images engender deep feelings of inadequacy and inexperience. Take heart! You can acquire as much, if not better, knowledge by cultivating your powers of observation. Local knowledge is, after all, merely a reservoir of practical information acquired over a long (or short) period of time. A century ago, many fishermen and experienced commercial sailors were illiterate. They learned their craft, their weather lore from years of hard-won experience based on acute observation. And this mind set of careful observation was inculcated into them from the moment they first went to sea.

Observation is a mind set—remember these words, dear reader, as you venture forth to anchor for the first time. This mind set involves looking at the sea and the land—not just as a view, but as a source of valuable information. Try sailing to windward in smooth water with an expert skipper at the helm, someone who has sailed locally for many years. Notice that his or her eye is constantly to windward, looking for telltale dark patches on the water, for inconspicuous riffles that signal a gust or a favorable wind shift. Meanwhile, your skipper plays the wind, never letting his or her powers of observation wander. His or her mind set concentrates on getting to windward as fast as possible, making use of all the inconspicuous landmarks and signs learned over years of sailing the same waters. Exactly the same mind set applies to anchoring, for it turns anchoring from a science into the art that it is.

It is this quality of careful observation that separates the anchoring artist and seaman from the novice. "How did she decide to anchor there?" you ask in impressive amazement, as the skipper chooses the perfect place in the sheltered bay, placing the yacht in just the right place to enjoy a cooling wind at night. Ten to one that he or she quietly watched the gentle gusts that darkened the water while the crew ranged the rode on deck.

Observation while anchoring comes into fullest play while selecting the anchorage. It is a matter of choosing the most sheltered cove or portion of an anchorage by consulting the chart and comparing what it tells you with the topography of the surrounding land. It is observing the behavior of yachts already anchored at your destination. How do they swing to the wind? Are they heeling to sudden gusts or lying to two anchors? Is everyone anchored to one side of the anchorage to avoid a tidal stream sluicing through the middle? There are many other such observations of this nature. They come from practical experience gained from using a wide variety of anchorages in an infinite variety of weather conditions. There is only one way to acquire such experience—by going out and anchoring for yourself.

LEARNING ANCHORING

Watching an anchoring maestro at work might tempt you to believe that acquiring the basic skills is difficult. Far from it. The basic routines and rules are easily learned if you make a systematic attempt to do so. Begin by shipping out with an experienced cruising skipper on a cruise when you know the boat will be anchoring several times a day, perhaps for lunch as well as overnight. Ask specifically for anchor handling experience, and try to work alongside an experienced foredeck hand who has the patience to take you through the routines and show you the little tricks that make all the difference. Once you have helped a few times, ask if you can do all the work, with your mentor watching and advising. The basic principles you learned in your reading will come alive, literally in your hands.

Once the foredeck is familiar territory, graduate to the cockpit, and ask the skipper to explain his reasoning while conning the ship into a new anchorage. Why anchor where we did? Why two anchors? What about the best depth? What did you learn from watching the water or from observing the other yachts in the anchorage? You will learn more by watching and asking questions than you will in any number of readings of this or any other book on anchoring.

When you have learned as much as you can from watching and asking questions, arrange to be the skipper for a couple of anchoring drills. The captain may stand by you, itching to grab the helm, but let his or her hoary head acquire a few more gray hairs! It's the only way you'll learn!

When your apprenticeship is over, go off on your own without anyone to help you out of trouble. Once you have taken the psychological plunge, practiced a few times in deserted bays, and anchored a couple of times in more crowded coves, you'll be well on your way to acquiring as rich an experience as any of the experts.

A final word of warning before we enter the world of anchors, rodes, and anchoring procedure. You can learn the basic rules of anchoring, the procedures for setting and recovering anchors, in a few hours. The rest is sheer, sometimes hard-won experience, and you should realize from the beginning that you will make mistakes and often when you first set off on your own. But every mistake, every hectic drama that creates a melange of anchor lines on the foredeck, separates you from those who have never anchored on their own. No part of cruising, whether under power or sail requires so much of you, is so intolerant of mistakes. The art of anchoring, and it is an art, is a matter of experience, and still more experience. Then, one day, you'll suddenly realize that you've tamed the beast, that you've acquired a level of confidence and experience that will always be there for you.

When I was sixteen, my ex-naval mentor handed me the helm as we felt our way into a tiny, rock-girt cove in western Sweden. "Anchor her," he said quietly, as we shortened sail. There was no diesel close to hand, only a tan genoa carrying us before the evening wind. A moment of sheer terror, my mind froze. Then, miraculously, the routine came into mind, hours of hard work hauling and sweating, watching others anchoring in seemingly inaccessible places. I swung the boat into the wind, let her fall back, called out "let go" in as authoritative a voice as I could muster. We snubbed in, paid out chain, and came to a stop. Hardly to my surprise, I realized I was gripping the tiller with whitened fingers. "Well done," said my mentor, as he clapped me on the back. The magic, the satisfaction, of that moment is with me still.

Welcome to the deeply satisfying world of anchoring!

CHAPTER TWO

Ground Tackle

"Men of War, East Indiamen, and large ships in the Southern Trade, carry one Sheet Anchor, one Spare Anchor, two Bower Anchors, one Stream Anchor, and one Kedge."

Darcy Lever, *The Young Officer's Sheet Anchor,*
Philadelphia edition, 1819.

I N THE DAYS OF SAIL and often unreliable, often smelly auxiliary engines, one's anchors were probably the most important gear aboard. Even today, when you can reach down and start a reliable diesel in a few seconds, shipping out with the right ground tackle is still of vital importance. Your preparations for safe anchoring begin long before you leave harbor, at fitting-out time.

GROUND TACKLE FOR COASTAL CRUISING

Despite all the mystique about crossing oceans, the fact remains that deepwater sailing is a relatively straightforward part of cruising, especially along trade wind routes. Coastal cruising is far more hazardous. One must cope with lee shores, tides, intricate navigation, steamer traffic — and anchoring. The stakes for a ship's gear are accordingly higher. Your depth finder may quit on you, a cherished genoa may rip, or the engine may fail, but you can still reach port. But a snapped anchor warp, a dragging anchor of inadequate weight, or a parting shackle can have immediate and catastrophic effects. The only way you can guard against such disasters is by shipping out with reliable, top quality ground tackle of adequate weight and size. Your entire ground tackle setup must work as a unit, or, to use more technical language, be an integrated system.

Your ground tackle requirements will depend on where you sail. A friend of mine who sails on England's Norfolk Broads carries simple grapnel anchors that can be dug into the bank in a few seconds. He also sails with a heavy concrete weight and a nylon rode, so he can anchor in open water. The worst that can happen to him is to drag into the reeds.

His ground tackle is perfectly adapted to local waters. At the other extreme, a blue-water crew will carry two or three anchors of different types, at least three rodes, or main anchor chain and two rodes, tripping line buoys, stoppers, and numerous spare anchor shackles. The yacht's anchor winch will be designed to handle heavy weights and brutal loads. The blue-water crew is prepared for any anchoring conditions and for every type of bottom from coral to deep grass and rock. The third anchor may never be used, but when it is needed, your boat's survival may be at stake.

The coastal cruising yacht may spend much of her time sailing in congested, shallow waters, but she is unlikely to meet extreme weather conditions other than those that one meets in the course of a normal summer. However, your ground tackle must be sized for the worst foreseeable conditions, however unexpected they may be, and be capable of handling the highest load conceivable and then some. Also, when making your selections, bear in mind that ground tackle can do far more than just anchor your boat. You can use it to haul yourself off a sandbank, warp the boat from one side of an anchorage to another, even to grapnel the bottom for fouled lines. Your ground tackle is one of the most versatile equipment systems you have aboard. More times than I can remember, I have used a kedge line to tow another yacht or to serve as a long warp in a crowded marina.

When choosing ground tackle, take the size and rig of your vessel into careful account. Boats with large surface areas, with tall masts, flying bridges, or with high cabins and topsides will need heavier anchors than normal to combat increased windage. Obviously, too, you will need heavier ground tackle if you cruise habitually in very windy areas, or where currents and tides run strong. You should also take careful account of the sea bed conditions near home, and in the areas you intend to cruise, for different anchor designs are at their best over different bottoms.

The coastal cruising yacht between 25 and 40 feet long should ideally carry the following ground tackle, all of it mutually compatible:

- Two anchors, the main anchor being usually heavier than the second (kedge) anchor. The bower should be the heaviest practical;
- Two anchor rodes made up of nylon line and short lengths

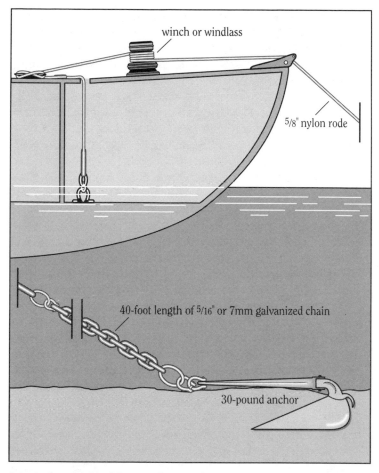

A typical ground tackle setup for a 25-foot to 35-foot cruising sailboat, utilizing chain and rode.

of chain, or alternatively, a main anchor chain and a kedge rode with a short length of chain;

- A spare warp that can serve as a rode in emergencies;
- Sufficient anchor shackles to fasten the rodes, chains, and anchors together, plus spares for each size. Seizing wire for the shackle keys is essential;
- A nylon bridle with eyes at each end for securing chain in the anchor locker (chain installations only);
- An anchor buoy and trip line, long enough to be used in the maximum water depth you normally anchor in;

- A sharp knife for emergencies;
- A pair of pliers or a crescent wrench to secure anchor shackles;
- Chafing gear for fairleads.

The yacht itself should be equipped with an adequate bow roller fairlead, strong cleats for securing lines, and a well-ventilated chain locker with a hawsepipe. The anchor wells found on many modern fiberglass yachts are ideal, provided they have good drains to remove water coming over the bows at sea. Larger vessels over 35 feet long should probably own a strong windlass, especially if they anchor in deep water or if the skipper or crew have a bad back.

ANCHORS

Every year brings more anchor designs to market and it is becoming increasingly hard to navigate between claim and counterclaim. Here are some well proven designs:

Fisherman-type anchors are the classic standby of yesteryear. Few modern anchor designs rival them for excellent holding under almost any conditions. Unfortunately, fisherman anchors are cumbersome to handle and difficult to stow. Their vertical blades foul anchor lines with great eagerness. Their holding qualities depend on the shape of the flukes, normally triangular or diamond-shaped. Once dug in and set with ample scope, the fisherman is a wonderful storm anchor. It is even effective on rocky bottoms. I have used a fisherman with great success on grassy surfaces, for its long arms need only a small gap in the bottom to hold. The Herreshoff or Luke design with diamond-shaped flukes is about the best—if you can find one. (The Luke anchor is manufactured by Paul E. Luke, Inc., East Boothbay, ME 04544.) The effectiveness of a fisherman depends on the length and weight of *chain you* use with it.

Many long-distance cruisers carry a fisherman anchor as a hurricane hook, stowing it in the bilge or on the cabintop with the stock collapsed along the shank. You should be careful to wire the securing pin of the collapsible stock in place while the anchor is in use.

Not enough coastal cruising yachts ship out with a fisherman anchor, partly because you have to use a much heavier anchor to achieve the same holding power as you can obtain with other types. I think the fisherman is an ideal backup anchor, purely on the grounds of its versatility and proven design.

Plow anchors are the favorites of many cruising sailors, whether bound for blue water or sailing close inshore. The classic design is the *CQR*, but in recent years various manufacturers have attempted to improve on this most effective of anchors.

Professor Geoffrey Taylor designed the CQR (acronym for "secure") for flying boats (seaplanes) in 1933. A hinged plowshare at the end of a long shank is so designed that the point tends to dig into the bottom, even when the blade is on its side. Combine the CQR with a long chain or rode, and the digging-in qualities are enhanced still further.

Having anchored thousands of times with plow anchors, I am convinced there is nothing to touch them on every kind of bottom except weed and hard rock. Unlike the fisherman, they are almost impossible to foul and offer a very favorable weight-to-holding power ratio. CQRs are reluctant to drag, even when provoked. Many times in my experience when one has dragged, I have let out more rode and the anchor has dug in again. This doesn't always happen, but the tendency to dig in when scope is added is a comforting quality.

The CQR has few disadvantages. The shape is cumbersome, but the stock slides easily into a bow roller, which is where most people secure it with a bolt. If you have to bring a CQR aboard, you can fold the blade over and put it in deck chocks with ease.

If you buy a CQR, be sure that you purchase a drop-forged one. They provide the correct strength and are properly balanced. Beware of cheap imitations, and *never* purchase one the shank of which detaches from the blade with a pin. This merely adds another weak spot.

Some of the new generation of plow anchors build on hard-won CQR experience. Of these designs, by far the best and most versatile is the *Delta* anchor, manufactured by Simpson-Lawrence, who also make the CQR.

The Delta is a new generation one-piece plow anchor without moving parts, with a delta-shaped blade (whence the name) and a shank so fashioned that it can be self-launched, free-falling, from a stowed position. The same shank design ensures that the anchor will immediately try to right itself, owing to the extreme "apex" ballasting and geometric figuration of the design. A low center of gravity and high

Common anchor designs

BRUCE

FISHERMAN

DANFORTH

CQR

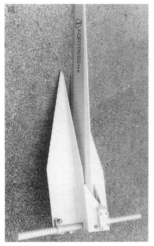

FORTRESS

DELTA

stability ensure that the anchor hits the seabed in the natural setting position. Thus, the anchor sets rapidly, without the need for massive tugs to flip it over. Once set, the blade is designed to provide a balanced hold in the seabed, which ensures both stability and exceptional holding power with only modest weight. The fixing eye fits all universal chain and rope end fittings. Simpson-Lawrence recommend a minimum of 16 feet of chain and 5x scope on the rode.

I have been using a 22 lb Delta for some time on my 34-foot sloop, mainly on sandy and grassy bottoms, in wind strengths from flat calm to 35 knots. My Delta sets impressively fast when snubbed, or even when not. Diving friends tell me it digs in even in calm conditions. I have not anchored, however, in fast-running tidal situations where the anchor might have to reset itself through 180 degrees. But judging from the ease of set, this kind of situation should not be a problem. The Delta is a nicely designed, very versatile anchor that is remarkable for its ease of setting and handling. Its superior setting ability makes it a natural choice for the serious cruising sailor.

The *Danforth* anchor was developed by American designer R. Danforth in 1939. Its blades are hinged to the shank. Whichever way the anchor falls to the bottom, the points will bear downward. A long stock runs across the base of the blades, helping tip them at an angle of about 30 degrees to the bottom, so they can dig in.

Ideally, the stronger the pull on a Danforth, the more the blades dig in. But this does not always work, especially if they skip over a hard bottom as the vessel moves astern. I have found that once Danforths drag, they will not reset until you start all over again. Their holding qualities are excellent under normal conditions, although, to obtain equivalent holding power, a Danforth must be much heavier than a plow. Like the CQR, the Danforth is poor on weed.

I use a Danforth as a kedge, in which capacity it serves well except when it hooks under a rock. When that happens, you need divers to clear it.

There are many Danforth anchors in the market, but I think the very best are made by West Marine, who have taken the trouble not to cut corners, use a precision crown to position the anchor at exactly the right angle, and a proper die-cut, tapered shank. Their Performance brand is superb.

The *Bruce* anchor was developed in 1972 for offshore oil

rigs. The manufacturer claims that it can rotate through 360 degrees without coming out of the bottom, also that the Bruce sets in a shorter distance over the bottom than any other design. Smaller versions are now widely seen on cruising yachts. The Bruce is basically a curved plowshare with three blunt flukes and an L-shaped shank. It is designed to hit the bottom with its weight resting on one fluke. As the anchor is pulled along, the fluke digs in. Like all anchor designs, the Bruce has its advocates, many of whom swear by its holding properties under gale conditions. Many people cruising the South Pacific rely on the Bruce, for it acts as a grapple in coral and grabs readily in sand and on rocky bottoms. It has also proven very effective in Southern California anchoring conditions, where one encounters sand, clay, and scattered rock outcrops.

There are many other anchor designs, each with their passionate followers. The *mushroom anchor* is ideal for permanent moorings, for the cup-like base with its vertical shank tends to oscillate on the bottom. If the sea bed is soft, the anchor will sink ever deeper into the mud, to the point that it can provide up to ten times its weight in holding power. Widely used by small fishing boats in sheltered lakes, they are not suitable for day-to-day cruising yachts requiring more horizontal anchor sets. The aluminum *Fortress anchor* is a pivoting fluke design, with the flukes bolted to the stock. These are lighter weight anchors, widely used by light displacement racing yachts and small cruising vessels, which can be adjusted to 32 and 45 degree fluke angles for use on sand or mud bottoms. I must confess they make me nervous because there are bolts on the sea bed which could (at least theoretically) work loose. They also lack the weight to penetrate clay and grass. If you choose a Fortress, be sure to mate it with chain and rode of equivalent weight for a conventional steel anchor of the same size. Simple *grapnel hooks* are widely used to secure to canal and river banks, while the so-called *flying anchor*, secured aboard in a bag complete with line is said to be capable of holding your boat merely by being cast out ahead of the bow. I have no first-hand experience of these anchors, but some German sailors swear by them.

No two sailors will agree on the right combination of anchors for their boat. Personally, I favor a combination of a CQR, or Delta as the main anchor and a Danforth as a kedge. Others argue that a Danforth or Bruce as primary anchor and a

Danforth as kedge will serve you well in most coastal cruising situations. Best listen to those who have cruised locally for a while and follow their advice. Be conservative until you have anchored many times! Trying unproven designs is best left to experts who feel like a change! If you plan any even mildly serious cruising, ship out with a third anchor, too, a fisherman in the bilge. As for recommended weights, the accompanying table gives some suggestions—but be guided by local conditions, especially the holding ground available in your home waters. If in doubt, follow the age-old cruising sailor's rule: "Take the maximum weight, then add more."

Lastly, don't forget a small dinghy anchor. A small Danforth or stockless anchor is ideal.

CHAINS AND RODES

The great "chain versus rode" debate rages wherever small-boat sailors congregate, with no resolution in sight.

Chain has several immediate advantages. Its heavy weight settles on the bottom and delivers a better horizontal pull to the anchor, as well as needing less scope (about 4:1). A great length of chain gives much greater elasticity to the cable and prevents violent snubbing (the jerking of a boat at her anchor at short stay), even under extreme conditions. Chain will not break suddenly. Rather, it will elongate, then break slowly—but I hope you are never in such a situation! Chain is abrasion-proof, propeller-proof, and coral-proof—no small considerations. It offers much greater security in deeper anchorages, and reduces swinging circles. Your yacht will sail around less in windy anchorages, too. But chain is heavy, sometimes monumentally so, when you haul your dangling cable up from 60 feet of water. It is also hard on the hands, especially when under strain. Gloves are essential and a windlass desirable. Yes, chain out of control can injure the unwary, so the crew must become aware of its whims.

If you decide on chain for your bower anchor, be sure to buy marine grade galvanized chain (or stainless steel if you are incredibly affluent). You will receive marine grade automatically if you order through your chandler. A 25- to 30-footer will usually ship out with $5/16''$ chain; with larger yachts, up to 44 feet long, use $3/8''$.

Until a few years ago, most serious sailors would have argued in favor of all that weight, on the grounds that they would sleep better at night. But the technology of modern synthetic ropes are such that you can now safely ship out with a chain and rode combination. The great strength/weight ratio and elasticity of today's nylon rode effectively eliminates the concerns over staying power that were reasonable some years ago—provided you set your anchor properly.

Chain and rode are now the preferred combination for most people, especially on yachts under 40 feet overall. The anchor is attached to a short length of chain, which in turn is shackled into an eye splice with a thimble in the nylon rode. The chain is essential, for it provides some badly needed weight on the bottom, resists abrasion, and gives a more horizontal pull on the anchor. Such a pull buries the anchor deeper and cuts down on snubbing. With nothing but a nylon rode, the pull is directed toward the surface, and the anchor tends to break out. The weight of the chain also allows the yacht to swing without pulling out the anchor. Short lengths of chain should be used on both your rodes.

How much chain should you fit? A minimum of 36 feet, even on a smaller yacht, is desirable. Personally, I prefer 40 to 50 feet to provide some real weight on the bottom, with about 30 feet on the kedge line. Chain sizes should coincide with those from an all-chain specification.

A good compromise in determining your rode system is to use as much chain as for normal anchoring conditions in your area, with the balance being line. This gives you all the advantages of chain, but substantial savings in weight and cost. An example would be 120 feet of chain with 230 feet of line. It would be rare to use more than the chain, but if very strong winds and seas arise, you can let out plenty of scope.

Another option is to use hi-tensile chain rather than proof coil or BBB. (Proof coil and BBB are of similar breaking strengths. BBB has more chain links per foot and is usually used for an all chain system because there are more links engaged by the windlass than with the longer proof coil links. BBB is more expensive, so many systems are of proof coil.) In general, hi-tensile chain is two sizes stronger than proof coil or BBB. Thus, a 35 foot boat could use ¼" hi-tensile chain for about the same cost and with less weight in the bow than if standard ⁵⁄₁₆" chain were selected. But the strength of the ¼" chain is two sizes larger or about the same as ⅜" chain.

Nylon rode has the great advantage of elasticity. It should be of sufficient diameter for comfortable handling, with or without gloves. On most yachts, this means at least ½", preferably larger. Three-strand lines are best, having high breaking strengths and superior chafe-resisting qualities. You can also splice broken lines if you have to.

Dacron line should not be used for anchoring. While it is about the same strength as nylon, it has very little stretch and, as such, does not provide the shock absorption characteristics at anchor that nylon does.

Nylon braid does not have the "memory" of three strand. Three strand usually must be coiled the same direction each time to avoid tangling, while braid does not. This is a useful attribute when the rode must be passed through a hawse pipe and it is not easy to reach the anchor locker to ensure that the line is stacking properly.

Carry as much line as you can, and then some more. Even on a 30-footer yacht where 30 feet is a common anchoring depth, you should carry a minimum of the following:

- a 180- to 240-foot main anchor warp;
- a 180-foot kedge warp;
- and a 120-foot backup warp of the same dimension as your anchor lines.

These rode lengths are over and above your short length of chain.

Before using either chain or rode, mark them at regular intervals. Paint several chain links at 30-foot intervals, either with different colors or with, say, one link painted at five fathoms, two at ten, and so on. Make sure the code is readily understood. Nylon rodes are best marked with whippings or pieces of line threaded through the strands. The pretty nylon labels available in marine stores look nice for a year or so, but are soon tattered by regular use. Besides, it is easier to feel whippings in bad light than to peer at faded lettering.

SHACKLES AND BRIDLES

Anchor shackles are the potential weak links in any ground tackle. The size you fit is limited by the size of your chain and anchor eye. If the shackle is galvanized, try to make its diameter at least 30 percent larger than that of the chain; stainless steel shackles should be of the same diameter as the chain. The latter are preferable, as they reduce the risk of corrosion. It is

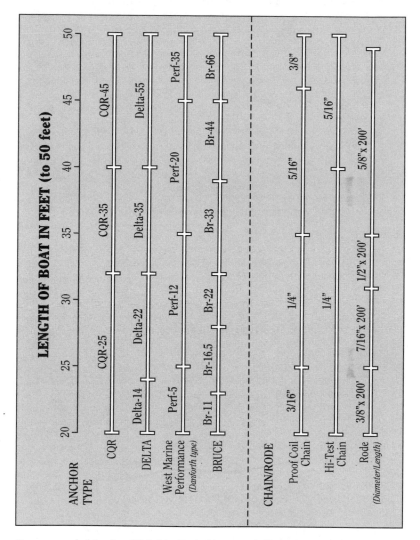

*Recommended Anchor Weights, Rode Sizes, and Chain Sizes
for Yachts Between 20 and 50 Feet Overall. (Courtesy West Marine)*

best to make all your shackles on both anchor lines the same size, then carry at least two spares aboard. You will need them when you least expect them.

When assembling the ground tackle, tighten the shackles with pliers, but take care to lubricate the pin with waterproof grease so you can free it in a hurry. Then wire the pin tight so that it can never come apart underwater. Check the pin and the lashing every time you bring the anchor on board. Some sailors use plastic wire ties, especially when the anchor and chain are routinely separated for storing.

Many sailors now splice their rodes to the chain. This has the advantage of easing passage through the hawsepipe. where a shackle can jam at a critical moment. However, a splice into the end link at a chain means a very small eye in the splice. A stronger arrangement is to splice the rode into a thimble, giving a bigger eye, and then to shackle the thimble to the anchor ring. A clever trick is to install shrink tube over the splice, which reduces the risk of chafing and helps keep the splice intact.

The standard way to tie a rode directly to the ring of an anchor is with the anchor or fisherman's bend, which is simply

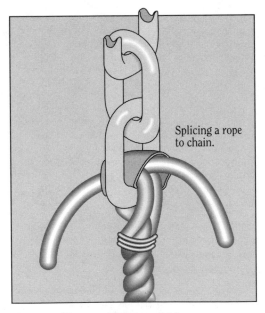

Splicing a rope to chain.

Courtesy Simpson-Lawrence Ltd.

an extra round turn through the ring finished off by two or more—preferably more—half hitches It's not a bad idea to seize the end back onto the standing part of the rode. Most people agree that using a shackle is best.

An anchor bridle is unnecessary for chain-and-rode ground tackle, because the nylon rode acts as a shock absorber to reduce snubbing, but is essential for all-chain arrangements. Measure the distance from the securing eye in your chain locker to the middle of the foredeck. Then make a strong two-eyed nylon bridle of this length. Secure one end to the bitter end of the chain, the other to the eye in your locker. The shackles should be as strong as those underwater. The nylon bridle should be of equivalent breaking strength to the chain. If an emergency occurs, you can let out (veer) all the chain and

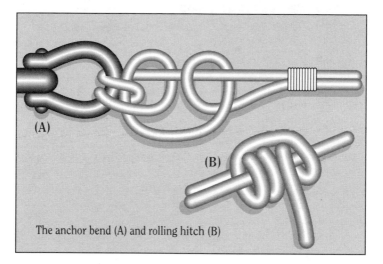

The anchor bend (A) and rolling hitch (B)

simply cut the bridle on the foredeck, without tunneling hastily into the chain locker.

Some experts like a much longer bridle, so they can put all the weight of the chain on the bottom. This is a matter of personal preference for coastal sailors. If you do without a bridle, lash the bitter end of the chain to the chain locker eye with a very strong nylon lashing, accessible enough to cut through quickly with a knife. *Do* not secure it with a shackle. When fastened at the base of the bobstay, an anchor bridle can serve to prevent chafing of the anchor line or chain against the bowsprit or bobstay.

BUOYS, LIGHTS, AND MISCELLANEA

In these days of congested anchorages and harbors choked with moorings, some form of anchor buoy is frequently very desirable. You can make use of a plastic bleach bottle, or better still, buy a plastic mooring buoy with a loop on the top. Paint the word ANCHOR on it, in case some clown comes along and tries to pick it up. Keep the buoy in a cockpit locker with a long length of lightweight line. The line is bent onto the crown of the anchor, or, when slipping your cable, to the bitter end of the chain or rode. To prevent a ghastly tangle, have a crew member on the foredeck holding the buoy and line clear to the bow roller side and away from the lifelines. As the anchor is let go, he or she casts the buoy and line well clear of the bow, so they do not foul the rode. (It is worth noting that an anchor buoy line can be used sometimes to raise a fouled anchor).

"A vessel of less than 50 meters in length may exhibit an all-round white light where it can best be seen..." The International Rules for the Prevention of Collision at Sea require all yachts under 50 meters (164 feet) overall to carry an all-round white anchor light at night, where it can best be seen. Masthead lights are fine, but are often too high to be readily seen at deck level by an approaching small boat. Some sailors prefer a special anchor light hoisted halfway up the forestay. A downhaul to the base of the lamp prevents the light from swinging. You can buy electric lamps to plug into a special socket on the foredeck. Even better are battery-powered lanterns with photoelectric cells that switch on and off automatically at dusk and dawn. Anchoring without lights in anything but the most remote anchorages is downright dumb, apart from being illegal.

By law, everyone is supposed to display a large black ball on the forestay when at anchor in daylight. Most yachts ignore this requirement, as it seems to be overkill. I have never known someone to be ticketed by the Coast Guard for this infraction.

Adequate chafing gear is another must. Some people carry leather rolls, others rely on lengths of plastic hose, and many yachts use old rags or toweling. You can also buy pre-assembled chafe kits at many chandleries. Whatever you use, be sure to carry plenty of it, with enough twine to secure it in place. A couple of hours in a windy anchorage will soon find the weaknesses in your ground tackle. Even modest gusts can chafe through the strongest ropes. I recommend putting chafing gear in place even on the calmest of nights. At the least, it saves wear and tear on expensive anchor rodes.

I always carry a stopper, a length of line that I can attach to the rode or chain to take the strain while I move the cable to another cleat or from windlass to samson post. With a chain setup, the stopper is equipped with a chain hook. A rolling hitch secures it to a rode. This piece of equipment is invaluable if you are working with two anchors simultaneously. Incidently, most anchor winch manufacturers recommend against having their windlass carry the load of the chain over extended periods. They recommend that chain stoppers be used to relieve the windlass of continual stress on its gears and motor.

Some larger yachts—especially those with windlasses— are equipped with stout deck stoppers. These are an admirable piece of equipment. Fit one if you can.

Last, but not least, you should always carry a sharp knife, robust and keen enough to slice through an anchor rode at a moment's notice.

ON-BOARD INSTALLATION: FAIRLEADS, CHAIN LOCKERS, WINDLASSES

You should give as much thought to the deck installations for working your ground tackle as you do to the anchor systems themselves. For example, how will you secure two anchors from the bow? What winches would you use if you had to careen your boat off a sandbank, a maneuver that requires canting the masthead over about 35 to 45 degrees? Having once taken three hours to unglue a 40-footer from a clinging Bahamian sandbank, much of it spent improvising leads to halyard winches, I can testify to the importance of advance preparation.

Here are the basic ingredients of a good deck system:

- Double bow rollers on *both* sides of the forestay. These should have bronze or stainless steel rollers. The roller should be wide enough to remove the cable (anchor rode or chain) in a hurry, and the sides should be high enough to keep the cable from jumping out when under strain from an angle. With chain, some form of ratchet pall arrangement on the roller is wonderful, but usually a windlass will provide this. Many smaller production yachts are fitted with just single anchor rollers. Fit a second one if you can.
- Strong cleats on either side of the bow, placed well clear of

Good bow rollers.
An essential feature
of all serious cruising
yachts, whether
power or sail.

warp fairleads and providing good leads for anchor rode tie-offs. These can double as mooring cleats. If you have chain, and even if you have rode, some form of samson post strengthened below decks or leading right down to the keel is desirable, if not essential. The old double samson posts found on older gaff-rigged yachts are ideal.

• A windlass is a wonderful device—especially the old, chain-eating manual windlasses that would move feet of chain at a stroke. Windlasses are essential on yachts longer than about 36 feet, and even on smaller ones if you are using all chain.

The market is crowded with manual, hydraulic, and electric windlasses. I would go for robustness, simplicity of design, and speed under load. The power source is a matter of personal preference. There is no substitute for a good manual windlass on a smaller yacht between 25 and 45 feet. Most are double-action forms, so you can pull up chain on both the fore and aft stroke. Two speeds are essential for speed, with a low gear for rough weather and when breaking loose the anchor. Some of the smaller British Simpson-Lawrence designs are superb, as are models from Lofrans, Muir, Vetus, and Maxwell. The Simpson-Lawrence manual windlass has a special patented gypsy that is designed for combination rode/chain installations.

Hydraulic windlasses work by oil pressure and generally require elaborate installations. They are rarely found on yachts under 45 feet long. They are very efficient and are a good choice if your boat has other hydraulic equipment on board that can use a common electric pump.

Many people fit electric windlasses, and I have found them reliable even under the most arduous conditions. However, you should install one with adequate circuitry, a circuit breaker that snaps off in case of excess load from a fouled anchor, and easily accessible controls. The ideal is a waterproof foot control near the operator's foot on the foredeck. Remote control systems are good for short handed sailboats, but are more frequently found on powerboats where operation from the bridge provides good vision. Some even have remote systems for deploying stern anchors, which strikes me as the ultimate in gadgetry!

Winches can be self-tailing or not self-tailing, horizontal or vertical. Non self-tailing winches are most common and are operated from the foredeck, for you have to tail the rode as it comes home. They also have the advantage that you can take turns around the gypsy and control the line when it is flowing out.

Anchor locker recessed into the foredeck with windlass and foot control (right). Such installations are commonplace on modern sail and power yachts.

Self tailing winches are used mainly on larger yachts and on powerboats. They allow you to power the rode or chain both up and down, the latter being somewhat of a slow process, requiring you to keep the boat right over the anchor for longer than usual. Some designs, notably the Simpson-Lawrence series, allow the anchor almost to freefall, handle both chain and rode, and even have chain counters, so you know how much you have over the bow.

Unless you use warp alone, you should buy an anchor windlass with both winch drum and chain gypsy (an auxiliary drum on the end of the windlass). The traditional windlass is a horizontal design, with the chain gypsy to starboard. I find these easier to operate, especially when coping with wraps when lines or chain are under strain. Vertical windlasses are more compact and take up less space. With the improved technology of recent years, they are generally the winch of choice on normal cruising yachts, with the advantage that the interior motor is less exposed to the elements.

The selection of a windlass depends upon the configuration of the boat's bow, its anchor locker, the type of rode selected, and the capacity required. Often the physical dimensions of the bow layout will limit what type and model of windlass can be fitted. If the bow roller is mounted very high, often a vertical windlass will not work unless it is mounted on a substantially elevated block. In such a case, a horizontal windlass is usually the best choice. (The axis of rotation of the windlass drum is vertical on a vertical windlass and horizontal on a horizontal windlass.)

Type of rode—all chain, mostly chain, or mostly line—is a major factor in selecting a windlass. If the rode is primarily line, it is easier for the operator to use a horizontal windlass. He or she can stand erect and easily tail the line coming off the windlass. In the case of a vertical windlass with line as rode, the operator may have to kneel or sit to align the line coming off the windlass. For the most part, use a horizontal windlass for a mostly line rode system. Use a horizontal or vertical for mostly chain and all chain. Whichever you choose, try to find a windlass that operates at both fast and slow speeds. Nothing is worse than cranking in 60 fathoms of chain at slow speed. And nothing is more lethal than changing from rode to chain in midstream, especially when a strong wind is blowing.

With regard to capacity, check the manufacturers' tables for boat size and prevailing winds expected to determine the pounds of pulling force needed. This is a somewhat subjective decision, because some boating areas require only casual anchoring, and others require very serious anchoring in severe conditions. The size selection also depends on whether the windlass will be used under certain conditions to pull the boat forward in high winds or whether it will only be used to break the anchor loose and pull up the weight of the anchor and rode. If in doubt, consult a good chandler, talk to local boaters, and observe the systems on well found boats. A windlass is not a piece of equipment you order casually from a discount mail order house!

Once you have calculated the type of windlass and desired size you think you need, consult your chandler's stock and his catalogs to see what is available. You will find that the various manufacturers do not have the same capacities, dimensions, and prices. Your final decision will be a result of finding the best fit taking these characteristics into consideration. This is an area where expert advice is essential, for the products on the market change constantly, reflecting constant innovations and improvements.

When installing your windlass, pay careful attention to the lead from the hawsepipe. The cleaner this lead the less frustration you will suffer over the years. Many designs now

Vertical windlass installation.

expect you to fit the anchor winch inside the deck anchor locker. I may be conservative, but I vastly prefer to have the winch on deck, where there is more space to work around it, and where it is accessible when an override or jam occurs. In my experience, winches set in wells seem to jam more than those on deck, but maybe I am biassed. Anchor lockers should be located directly below the windlass, should provide a good gravity drop for the rode, and should be large enough to accommodate it without the need to reach in to clear the accumulating line as the anchor is raised. This is ideal, but unfortunately too rare on modern boats. The design pressures on production builders to provide the largest possible forward stateroom has all too often resulted in inadequately designed and sized anchor lockers that do not allow enough drop for a self stowing line. As a result, it is sometimes necessary to make major changes to the locker when a serious anchoring system is needed.

- Chain lockers come in many shapes and sizes, everything from anchor wells set into the foredeck to full-blooded lockers in the forepeak where chain can stow itself as it's fed below. Anchor wells are ideal for the coastal cruiser provided the lids are strong and easily opened. You can snake the rode down into the open well, ready for use the next time.

  Snaking an anchor rode into a below-decks chain locker can be a time-consuming and irritating task when the spray is flying. A large-diameter hawse opening helps, but you should have one with a close-fitting cover, or carry a good waterproof plug aboard to keep green water out. Chain should self-stow below decks, but you may occasionally have trouble with twisting. Your only cure is to remove all the chain from the locker, undo it at the bitter end, and start all over again—not an edifying prospect in gale conditions.

- Kedge stowage is a common problem, especially on smaller yachts. All too often, this priceless piece of equipment ends up at the bottom of a cockpit locker in a jumble of other gear. You can flake down the rode into a plastic crate or bucket, with the chain on top. This is nearly failsafe, as is a drum mounted on the afterdeck, if you have one. Some people install the drum below decks and use a crank to feed the rode down a special hawsepipe. You are probably better off stowing the kedge itself on the aft pulpit. The stainless steel brackets sold for the purpose are excellent. You can then attach the rode without removing the anchor from its brackets.

The Ankarolina, a nifty device from Sweden, has been on the market for some years, a reel that you attach to your stern pulpit, with a webbing line that serves as your kedge warp. The line is directly to hand, never tangles, and can be wound up rapidly with the handle provided. They have gained wide acceptance in Europe, but people over here have been reluctant to embrace them, perhaps because they are unaware of the strength of nylon webbing. Webbing is, of course, easier on the hands than rope, but may tend to "float" more when being let out, which takes some getting used to.

- If you prefer to keep your bower anchor on deck, you should install some strong deck chocks. Special aluminum, bronze, or stainless steel brackets with holes for securing lines are sold for this purpose. The best ones have a bolt that runs through the chock and the anchor ring, securing it in any sea. If your anchor lives in the bow roller, you should install a push pin to keep the blade in place even in a heavy swell.

It's true that your ground tackle is only as strong as its weakest link. So careful preparation before you ever set foot in any anchorage will ensure smoother sailing and far fewer worries at night!

CHAPTER THREE

Choosing an Anchorage

"Anchorage may be obtained in westerly winds to the lee of the point, with the watchtower bearing 075 deg. Mariners are advised that the holding ground in this vicinity can be unreliable."

Mediterranean Pilot, 1887.

YOU CAN HAVE THE BEST ground tackle in the world, but it is ineffective if you do not use it competently. Just as importantly, you must select your anchorage with the greatest care and foresight. How many uncomfortable nights have I spent rolling unbearably when the wind shifts, simply because I did not bother to think ahead or listen to the forecast. Far more often than I am prepared to admit, so this chapter tries to discuss some of the variables in choosing that perfect anchorage.

For all their modern, often spartan appearance, most of the charts we use were originally surveyed by tough seamen working in small, open boats. They had sails and oars, a lead-and-line, and infinite patience. You can be sure that they knew the qualities of a good anchorage when they found one. That's why some of the old nineteenth century pilot books are so useful. They were written by small boat sailors for small boat sailors. I once found a completely deserted, absolutely sheltered anchorage on the west coast of Corsica simply by reading an old edition of the *Mediterranean Pilot*. It was not even mentioned in the local cruising guide. We weathered a 40-knotter in perfect comfort with just seagulls for company. So—start with the charts. It's a great pity that much small boat information is vanishing from government publications. Invest in the old ones while the going's good!

Choosing an anchorage begins with your charts, pilots, and local cruising guide long before you leave port. Look at the anchorages on the chart. Do they offer shelter from the prevailing winds? Read about your general destination in the cruising guide, if any. What does it say about holding ground, depths, and tidal conditions? Jot down some notes about potential anchorage choices, then list them in order of priority.

Whatever anchorage you choose, be sure to have one or two alternatives up your sleeve.

When selecting an anchorage, you must take psychological variables into account as well. How long a passage do you want that day, and how far do you want to travel the next? Do your crew members want a shore run in the evening, or do they prefer solitude, sandy beaches, or snorkeling or diving reefs? An experienced skipper balances cruise plans with seamanship. This is particularly important if you are on a bareboat charter in a cruising ground like the Virgin Islands, where there are so many subtle, and not-so-subtle delights ashore. No sane skipper neglects to visit the Bitter End, for the dinghy sailing, if not dinner ashore. Yet at least one night of solitude and complete quiet is the best medicine of all.

Your chart is a mine of information on shelter, depths, and good anchorages, many in the most unexpected places. Read the cruising guide first, but realize it is a conservative source. Anyone who compiles such a volume knows that the book must cater to people with limited experience, so both advice and sailing directions tend to be middle-of-the-road, and often downright cautious. Fellow sailors can also help, but understand that they have their own preferences and biases. A chart is dispassionate and accurate. Peruse it with the prevailing winds and swells in mind. Look closely at headlands and bays, and at the orientation of the land. Is there shelter behind a point? Do soundings indicate a sheltered pool close inshore, tucked away from the surge, with good holding ground? Are there tidal streams that flow through the cove, causing sharp wind-against-tidal popple? Choosing an anchorage is a delicate balance of many, sometimes subtle variables, everything from prevailing wind directions to the mate's passionate need for a morning swim.

When consulting charts, consider the following factors:
- Prevailing wind direction and force, and the weather forecast. Visualize the anchorage in relation to the wind in each quadrant.
- Directions of waves and swells.
- Holding ground.
- Length of proposed stay. A lunchtime stop is one thing, a stay of two weeks another.
- Likely visibility.

Chart Symbols Describing the Quality of the Bottom

Bottom type		Quality	
S	sand	c; crs	coarse
M	mud; muddy	h; hrd	hard
Cy; Cl	clay	so; sft	soft
G	gravel	sft	stiff
St	stones		
K	kelp	bl; bk	black
Wd	seaweed	wh	white
Grs	grass	yl	yellow
Rk; Rky	rock; rocky		
Co	coral		
Co Hd	coral head		
Sh	shells		

- Potential congestion in the anchorage.
- Distance to alternative anchorages.
- Local conditions, such as funneling winds or strong currents.

Once you have chosen an anchorage and several alternatives, consider these specific characteristics as follows:

- Difficulty of approach, with careful attention to day and night hazards, tidal and current sets, and visibility. It is unwise, for instance, to approach island reef passes in the South Pacific after 3:30 in the afternoon, when the sun is low.
- Soundings in the approach and within the anchorage. Observe how soundings cluster, and where pools of suitable depth lie.
- Local tidal streams and current patterns. Do these affect where you should anchor?
- Local topography, which can affect wind patterns. Anchorages below steep mountain valleys, for example, can bring the furies of downslope winds onto your head.

• Ease of escape during day or night if an emergency arises. Can you sail or motor to safely off a lee shore on a moonless night without having to use a depth sounder or consult a chart? If not, do prevailing conditions merit taking the risk of being unable to get out? (In many cases they do.)

If you are on an extended cruise, you may be interested in available shore facilities, such as stores, water supplies and mechanical help, if needed. It's a fair bet that most harbors will provide water and fuel, especially if they are fishing ports, but it is well to plan ahead, especially in Third World cruising grounds.

FINAL APPROACH

The first golden rule is to complete as much advance preparation work before you leave on passage, for the most important judgements still lie ahead. Your first Moment of Truth comes when you identify your chosen anchorage from afar and begin your approach.

The final approach to an anchorage begins when you sight landmarks for your destination. Even with all the advantages of GPS, Loran, and radar, approaching an unknown coast can be confusing, especially in reduced visibility. If you have even the slightest doubt about your location, take bearings from the landmarks to double-check your position. It is easy for headlands to look alike, especially when you are approaching at an angle different from that illustrated in a cruising guide. This is particularly true in low-lying cruising grounds, where you may be using such landmarks as churches or small villages to pilot your way along a featureless coast. The eastern Swedish coast is a good example, for the only landmarks are tall church steeples. It is easy to get lost, until you realize that the architects, perhaps out of pity for navigators, designed each steeple differently! And the pilot books actually illustrate them with small drawings. Once you've figured out how the locals do it, it's simplicity itself. One important point—as you shift from a small scale chart to a large scale coastal or harbor chart, remember that per-inch (or centimeter) distances on the latter chart are much less. At this stage, it's wise to double check the tide tables to get an idea what depths above chart datum to expect during the approach and the actual anchoring (see Chapter 9).

The most common approach hazards are subsurface rocks, coral reefs, and strong cross-currents. If the chart has approach course lines, follow them carefully in order to stay clear of outlying dangers. If there are no lines, meticulously identify the hazards and give them a wide berth, preferably to leeward.

As you close in, pass the helm over to another crew member, keep an eye on the course, and go forward to pinpoint the anchorage. Look at the local topography. Is the land high, with narrow valleys that funnel strong gusts into the anchorage? Can you anchor behind a low spit where the winds are always steady, or take advantage of updrafts to find shelter in the lee of a cliff? Become as familiar as you can with the features of the area, and, repeat the exercise on future occasions, until you know the spot like the back of your hand.

With the topography in mind, look astern. Is the approach easy to use at night? Could you slip your cable and sail (not motor) out on a moonless night? If not, consider going to another place where the escape route is safer, especially if weather conditions are changeable. Unfortunately, some of the best anchorages are tiny coves that seem cozy behind their rock-girt entrances. But they can be death traps when the wind blows from offshore. It's a matter of nice judgement and careful weather forecasting as to whether you can use them in settled conditions.

CHOOSING YOUR SPOT

As you approach the anchorage, you begin to confront the question of questions—where precisely shall I anchor? Before leaving port, you probably formed some opinions about the best spots. But close offshore you may find, for instance, that the tide is low or that a closely packed group of yachts occupy the best positions. Moorings that do not appear on the chart may clutter up the anchorage; kelp may infest the best spots. Despite problems and disappointments, you have to make an anchoring decision fast. This is when it is easy to become intimidated, and not to think logically. Stay calm, and carefully check the information at your disposal.

Look again at the prevailing wind and tidal conditions. How much of the anchorage offers enough depth for safe anchoring at all stages of the tide? Do wind gust patterns on the water show where shelter is best? With luck, you should be able to eliminate much of the anchorage area in a few moments of observation.

Then think about human hazards. Are there ferries or

seaplanes operating in the area? For example, Bimini in the Bahamas is legendary for its seaplanes, which land within yards of anchored sailboats. Does the cruising guide say anything about fishing, yacht racing, or water skiing? Have you, dear reader, ever anchored inadvertently in the middle of a Wednesday evening race course? You learn all kinds of new swear words! (To be fair to us, there was no way of telling that we had sinned.) Be aware of signs ashore with messages such as "Cable Crossing—Do Not Anchor." There may also be restricted areas off sandy beaches for swimmers. Again, the process of elimination comes into play.

Consider next where other vessels are anchored. Avoid mooring areas, where the bottom is invariably obstructed. Take a close look at other anchored yachts. Sailors tend to be gregarious and cluster in anchorages. Perhaps they feel safety in numbers, or maybe they assume that the first comers knew what they were doing. This may not be true! Do not be coaxed into joining the crowd before you figure out why others are anchored where they are. Oftentimes they may be clustered too far offshore, leaving a nice pool of clear water closer inshore. Go ahead and anchor there if you have a clear escape route. It's amazing how often you end up in a large, comfortable hole, simply because everyone else has just anchored without taking the time to scout out everyone's position first. The expert skipper takes time, circles through the anchorage several times, clears away ground tackle, *then* anchors.

As you circle carefully, check the wind and tide directions, decide which is stronger, and plan your approach so you end up bow to the stronger of the two.

At this point, you should choose one or two potential anchor spots. Turn on your depth finder and circle slowly around each one. Is there adequate depth at low water? Will you have enough room to put down sufficient scope, and to swing clear of your neighbors? Is there enough shelter where you want to anchor? This is the moment when you should double-check the lie of the anchor lines of other yachts, and whether others are secured with one anchor or two—these, by the way, can be laid from the bow or bow and stern. Be sure not to confuse someone's anchor buoy with a mooring, something which is a constant source of entertainment to idle spectators, but not to the careful skipper, who anchored ready for every eventuality except this one.

If you still have doubts—and such doubts are not uncommon in congested anchorages—circle around again. *If a safe berth still eludes you, divert to another anchorage.* It is safer to overnight at sea than to anchor on top of your neighbor without adequate safety margins. And if, after anchoring, you realize your berth has some flaw you overlooked, swallow your pride, search out a better spot, and move to it.

COPING WITH CONGESTION

As few as twenty years ago, you could anchor in well-known anchorages at the height of the season and still find plenty of room. Today, coping with congestion has become a way of life for many cruising sailors, even in remote areas such as the South Pacific. Congestion is irritating at the best of times, mostly because it forces you into close contact with your fellow sailors just when you crave peace and quiet. The only way to handle the problem is with extreme courtesy. Obey the rule that those who arrive first have priority—and the privilege of clear anchor lines. Most sailors are only too anxious to cooperate, and will do all they can to ensure you have enough swinging room. If you come across someone, as I once did, who threatened me with law suits if I even went near his boat, just smile and leave. Life is simply too short.

If the anchorage is congested, approach with great care, look for a vacant spot, then hover while you ask the neighboring yachts where their lines lie. You can rest assured that you'll hear quickly if you are about to foul someone else's line. If your neighbors offer help in laying out kedges, by all means accept, but remember that your own counsel is better than advice yelled from some yards away. Once you've anchored, row over and talk to your neighbors. Reassure them if they have worries about swinging room, and offer to move if they seem legitimately concerned. Apart from being a common courtesy, this is a wonderful way to meet fellow sailors!

One precautionary hint: if any yachts collide with yours, or if yours hits others, note the incident and damage in your log. This way, if damage claims arise, you can document the occurrence for your insurance company.

If in doubt about your ability to anchor safely, find another anchorage. Even on the calmest days, I always have an alternative up my sleeve, simply because there may be no space at your first choice. Southern California's offshore islands

"Coping with congestion has become a way of life for many sailors."

become chronically overcrowded on summer long weekends. On such weekends, I either stay home, or deliberately make for an unpopular anchorage, on the argument that most people won't try it. Sometimes this strategy works, sometimes it does not—so I always have a (usually) less desirable alternative in mind.

Finally, if you expect congestion, plan to arrive with enough daylight to reach another anchorage if necessary. On a recent Memorial Day, I made the mistake of leaving port too late in the day. We ended up groping our way into a tiny anchorage by flashlight. Fortunately, it was flat calm, but it was a lesson learned.

HURRICANE HOLES AND EMERGENCY ANCHORAGES

With luck, you will never have to weather a major storm or a hurricane at anchor. With careful timing and preparation, you can minimize such traumas. But deciding about shelter and good holding ground assumes new dimensions when survival is involved. Fortunately, modern satellite weather forecasts usually provide plenty of warning of hurricanes and other nastinesses.

When extreme weather threatens, you should head for the nearest anchorage that offers one thing above all else—

360-degree shelter from strong winds and swell. At issue is the question of "fetch," or the amount of open water that a wave crosses before it reaches you. In a small cove with a fetch of, say, 100 yards, the waves remain small no matter how strong the wind. But if the fetch in a bigger harbor is half a mile or more, sizable waves will build up in a storm. This is why most Caribbean hurricane holes are in the middle of mangrove swamps.

The ideal storm anchorage should also have superb holding ground, ample space for every sheltering vessel, and soft cushion-like shorelines—mangrove swamps are ideal—where your boat can blow ashore safely. You must also have adequate depth below your keel, allowing for sudden and dramatic water level changes that sometimes occur with exceptional tides. You must also be prepared for the eye of the storm, a period of disconcerting calm in the midst of the hurricane that precedes often even stronger winds.

The late Jay Bercaw, a sailor of vast experience, who sailed around the world twice with the legendary Irving Johnson, then circumnavigated in his ketch *Natasha*, was once near Fiji when hurricane warnings were posted. He made for an island hurricane hole and anchored as securely as he could in the middle of the bay. Several other yachts were there, including a new ketch from Hong Kong being sailed to the United States by her inexperienced owners. The wind came in so strongly that it sandblasted most of the varnish from *Natasha's* masts. Then came the lull as the eye of the storm passed over the snug bay. All was quiet. Everyone went on deck to check for chafe and to reset their lines in anticipation of what was to come.

Jay noticed that the ketch had dragged out to the mouth of the bay. To his astonishment, he saw no signs of frantic activity, as the owners took advantage of the calm to move back into shelter and reset their anchors. Instead, he was amazed to see the owner mounting his barbecue on the stern pulpit in preparation for a dinner to celebrate the passing of the storm. He leapt into his dinghy, told the skipper in no uncertain terms what was coming, and helped him move the ketch to shelter. The moral of the story is a simple one—know as much about weather extremes as you can before they strike.

Hurricane holes are few and far between on most coasts. It is worth gaining familiarity with local refuge places in calm weather, so you know which anchorage to make for if extreme weather conditions are forecast. And make sure that you get there well ahead of time, for you can bet that every boat within miles will be making for the same refuge.

Choosing the right anchorage may seem like a complicated process, and can be daunting, especially in rough weather or congested waters. But by exercising careful preparation and good common sense, you will soon gain the confidence to anchor safely in a wide variety of weather conditions.

CHAPTER FOUR

Basic Principles

"Anchoring is not a matter of learning esoteric engineering forces or of mastering catenaries. Rather, it is an art, acquired and practised in only one way—at the helm of your boat and on her foredeck."

John Peacemold Gruntfuttock, 1993.

THIS CHAPTER DESCRIBES basic anchoring routines and command procedures for dropping and recovering your anchor.

While the crew prepares the foredeck, the skipper sweeps through the anchorage scanning with the depth finder, as described in Chapter 3. Looking at several potential spots, escape routes, depths, and other yachts, he or she chooses the best location, juggling while he or she does so prevailing wind patterns and his or her knowledge of the tides. The skipper searches for the best shelter from wind and swell, for dinghy landing places and the best holding ground, as well as for safe depths. Once these choices are made, the anchoring routine begins.

"Prepare to Anchor"

This command marks the moment to prepare the decks for action:

- Start the engine, giving it ample time to warm up so it does not stop at an inopportune moment. Have you, dear reader, had your engine stall as you ease your way through a narrow, rock-girt channel with the current under you just as a merchant ship is coming toward you? I have, and it is not a situation conducive to peace of mind!
- Lower sail, leaving the main ready to be hoisted at a moment's notice if needed. The jib should be stowed clear of the deck, lashed to the rail if necessary, so it does not interfere with the ground tackle.
- Clear all clutter from the cockpit—beer cans, navigational equipment, sun hats, and so on. Coil sheets so they are not underfoot.
- Switch on the depth finder if you haven't already done so.

- Clear away the ground tackle. The foredeck crew loosens the anchor pin in the bow fairlead, and sets the anchor in place over the bow if necessary. They range all the chain and a good length of rode on deck, flaked so it will not muddle. (If you have just chain, bring some 20 feet (3 or so fathoms) on deck to make sure the cable runs freely.)
- In congested anchorages, have your second anchor ready to let go at short notice.
- Bring the dinghy close astern on a short line, or inflate the rubber boat on deck, and prepare it for use. (This is a worthwhile precaution in congested coves.) If you are towing an inflatable, bring it right up under the stern, even closer than a "hard" dinghy.
- Make sure every crew member is on station, ready to perform his or her assigned task.

It is essential that you brief every crew member about the anchoring approach. Quite apart from safety considerations, it gives everyone a sense of participating in the exercise.

"Approaching"

After giving this command, the skipper steers along the chosen approach line, if possible straight into wind and tide. The yacht reduces speed in good time, while the skipper checks depths and distances.

"Stand By"

The skipper is on final approach. This is the signal for the foredeck crew to ease the anchor to the waterline, readying it for release at a moment's notice. The yacht slows, then stops, and begins to drift astern.

"Let Go!"

Splash! The foredeck crew lets go the anchor. The chain and rode snake over the bow, controlled by a crew member with a turn around the windlass gypsy or a convenient cleat. As soon as the anchor has penetrated the bottom, the skipper puts the engine astern. The cable is laid out deliberately in as straight a line as possible.

"Snub!"

When a length of line three times the depth of the water is over the bow, the crew member at the cleat or windlass belays the rode or sets the brake on the chain. The yacht still courses astern while the crew watches the cable. It tightens and strains. The boat checks and turns to the line. The cable tightens, snubs, then relaxes.

While the crew checks the ship, the skipper comes forward to watch the line. If the anchor is set, all is well. If the line vibrates, indicating the anchor is bumping along the bottom, try letting out more scope to set it. If that fails, the entire anchoring process must start all over again.

Once satisfied the anchor is set by watching the land or other boats on the water to ensure backward movement is checked, the skipper should run the engine hard astern for half a minute or so to dig the anchor firmly into the bottom. By doing so, you reduce to virtually zero the chances of dragging in normal conditions. (Some experts believe this is unnecessary if the anchor is well set. I suspect it's a matter of personal preference.)

"Pay out scope."

The skipper is satisfied the anchor has dug in and specifies the amount of scope. The foredeck crew lets out the correct amount of scope by watching the marks on the anchor line until the proper mark is at the waterline. The yacht settles back into her correct berth, swinging to the wind. The crew belays the anchor line with adequate turns and a half hitch.

Everyone relaxes except the skipper. While the crew stows the mainsail, puts the dinghy over the side, and rigs the companion ladder, the captain watches the boat carefully. Is she swinging with the other yachts? Is the line snubbing and jerking? Check a couple of bearings on convenient landmarks ashore about every two or three minutes. If necessary, run the engine astern to make sure the anchor is not dragging. When you are at last satisfied, turn off the engine and secure the wheel or tiller. As a final precaution, note some bearings and the best night escape course in the log.

SCOPE

Scope, or the length of line between vessel and anchor, is a vital ingredient that determines the angle of pull on the anchor. More scope means a more horizontal rather than vertical pull and a better anchor hold. Decisions about scope depend entirely on the holding ground and the expected weather during the time of anchoring. Here are some general guidelines for

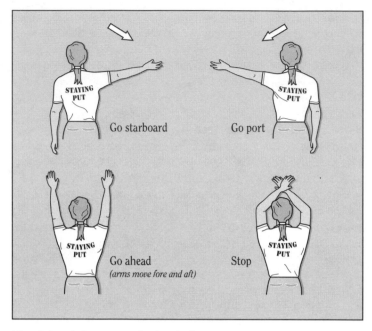

Hand signals for use on the foredeck

anchoring in depths up to 30 feet with chain (deeper water will get further attention later):
- In calm conditions with winds below 10 knots, lay out a length of line at least three times the depth of water.
- In winds between 10 and 25 knots, use line lengths at least five times the water depth.
- In 25- to 40-knot winds, pay out everything you've got, but use a line length at least seven times the depth.
- In winds above 40 knots, take special precautions, which we cover in Chapter 7.

These figures are for chain, and you should allow considerably more scope with rode. As a rule of thumb, increase the chain length-to-depth factors by two (5, 7, and 9 times for the wind speeds above, if there is space in the anchorage).

BUOYING THE ANCHOR

Buoying your anchor enables you to locate it and pull it to the surface if it hangs up on an obstruction. An anchor buoy marks the spot, attached by a tripping line secured to the crown of the

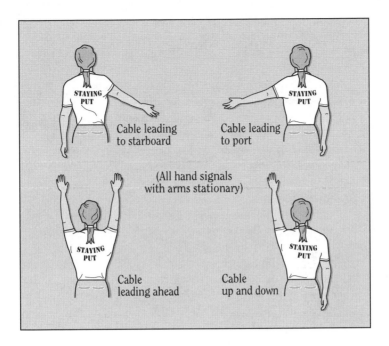

Cable leading to starboard

Cable leading to port

(All hand signals with arms stationary)

Cable leading ahead

Cable up and down

STAYING PUT

anchor. If you need to capsize the anchor to free it from an obstruction, simply recover the buoy and haul on the tripping line.

It is wise to buoy the anchor whenever you lie near moorings. Commercial harbors, coral reefs, and rocky bottoms are death traps for unbuoyed anchors. If the water is clear and you have scuba gear aboard, buoying is less important.

Be sure that you secure it to the crown alone, otherwise it will probably foul on the bottom.

HOLDING GROUND

The physical characteristics of the bottom, or "holding ground," are vital to secure anchoring. Sand is the ideal holding ground, except when it is very soft or extremely hard. I have known anchors to bounce over a hard sand bottom, too. Moderately firm clay is superb under normal conditions, but can be dangerous in a blow, when a jerking anchor can break loose in a lump of clay. I have known instances, too, where a lightweight anchor flips with the tide and brings up a lump of mud adhering to the fluke. The sticky lump prevents the anchor from digging in again and the boat drifts away down-tide. Nice, gooey mud is suitably glutinous and will hold a boat in any weather with the right scope. Gravel can be adequate, as can silt, but you should lay plenty of scope to compensate for the loose packing of the bottom.

Grass and seaweed offer uncertain holding at best. If your anchor is unable to penetrate the grass layer it will skitter along the bottom. Occasionally the flukes will catch a large tussock and hold until the wind picks up and jolts the anchor from its hold. If you must anchor on grass or seaweed, lay as much scope as possible and keep plenty of weight on the bottom.

Rocky bottoms are effectively useless for anchoring, while coral wreaks havoc not only with anchors, but with rodes, sometimes cutting through them in a few hours. And even the stoutest anchor winch will be unable to dislodge an anchor caught under a boulder or coral head. Avoid such areas if you can, but if you have to lie there, buoy your anchor with a tripping line, lay plenty of scope, use as much chain as possible, and try to pad your nylon rode where it touches the bottom. Stay clear of large heads and boulders, and keep scuba gear aboard. I once spent a very uncomfortable night over a coral patch just outside a comfortable harbor, simply because we couldn't recover our anchor without diving in full sunlight. It was stuck under a large rock.

You will notice symbols such as "Sh" (shell) or "Rk" (rock) alongside soundings on your charts. These general indications are helpful until you zero in on the anchorage, where details are too minute for inclusion on charts. You will do well to watch for changes in the water's color, especially in tropical areas. Caribbean and Bahamian waters are brilliantly colored, from intense white in shallow, sandy bays to turquoise and deep blue in deeper areas. With a little practice, you can guess the correct depth of water to within a foot or so just by judging bluish hues. Get into the habit of associating colors with depths by having someone call out depth readings from the cockpit instruments. You'll quickly become an expert that way.

In cloudy waters, some people carry an old-fashioned lead line, affixing in its hollow base some beeswax or a scoop of grease in order to bring up a bottom sample.

If you sail in very shallow waters like the British East Coast or the Florida Keys, you may find a painted pole the best kind of sounder. After all, if you go aground, you are most likely to go overboard and push! You can even buy a portable electronic depth meter these days, a stick-like artifact which you hold over the side. Maybe I am old fashioned, but I prefer the simplicity of a stick or lead and line...

WEIGHING ANCHOR

Under normal circumstances, weighing anchor is a simple routine. The wise skipper uses the same procedure each time, and delegates specific tasks to crew members.

"Prepare to weigh anchor"

At this formal or informal command, the skipper warms up the engine, the dinghy is brought aboard or taken on a short tow line, and the gangway ladders are stowed. The foredeck crew opens the anchor locker, and clears surplus ropes from the foredeck. Meanwhile, another crew member secures the cockpit and cabin for sea, putting away loose towels, empty bottles, and other clutter from the hours at anchor. Finally, the mainsail is prepared for hoisting on short notice, and the halyard is bent on. The skipper goes to the foredeck and checks on the lay of the anchor line.

"Hoist away"

On command, the foredeck crew hauls in the anchor line, calling out the line markers as they come over the bow. In moderate conditions, one person works the line while another flakes the slack below. The skipper stays at the engine controls and helm, waiting for signals from the bow that indicate when he or she should use power to approach the anchor and ease strain on the line.

As they haul in, the foredeck crew watch the anchor line closely. If it's slack, they haul in fast. As the cable begins to strain, they take a quick turn around the anchor cleat and wait until the line slackens. Simple hand signals are used to show the skipper which way to steer and how much engine power is needed to bring the boat up to the anchor with minimal line tension. An experienced crew can retrieve an anchor with slack on the line at all times. The judicious use of signals reduces confusion between bow and stern and minimizes uncontrolled shouting.

"Up and down!"

This all-important call from the foredeck means the cable is vertical. The anchor is ready to be broken out, or may already have left the bottom if there hasn't been much strain on it since it was set. This command is most important when getting the anchor under sail, for it tells the captain at which moment to steer the yacht toward the tack on which he or she wants to sail first.

"Up anchor!"

When the skipper gives this order, the foredeck crew hauls away hard, with every spare hand on the cable. Normally, the anchor breaks out easily, but everyone should be prepared for sudden heavy loads. If the anchor balks, take turns around a cleat or windlass and bring it in inch by inch, holding onto every gain. This way, the boat, rather than someone's arms, takes the strain. It's also important to hoist using your leg muscles and not your back, to minimize the risk of back injury.

Make sure you don't catch another yacht's anchor as you leave with yours still under the water. This is hilarious to watch—if your boat is not the one being carried out of the anchorage long before you are ready to leave!

"Anchor's aweigh!"

The foredeck crew calls out when they are sure the anchor is off the bottom. The skipper eases the yacht out of the anchorage under power, going slowly until the anchor is up and stowed. Meanwhile, the crew brings the anchor to the fairlead, washes off weed, mud, or sand, and secures the foredeck for passage.

Once the anchor is safely out of the water, stay in calm water until the foredeck crew has finished their work. Nothing is worse than playing with ground tackle as spray hits the deck, or setting sail with anchors underfoot.

These commands may seem superfluous in calm weather, but they are essential in rough conditions.

Hand signals are vital when 30 knots of wind is blowing over the deck, in which case even a loud shout is fragmented. Whenever raising anchor, insist that only the skipper and one foredeck hand call out, and use hand signals whenever possible. Caterwauling voices are guaranteed to raise passions and tempers, as well as entertain your neighbors. Another solution is headsets and intercoms, but I doubt if many smaller yachts go to this extreme.

SAFETY PRECAUTIONS

Few maneuvers offer a greater potential for disaster than anchoring. I have seen fingers crushed in bow fairleads, ankles sprained from careless stepping on moving anchor chains, and more stubbed toes than I can remember— including my own. Most of these accidents occurred in moderate weather, often because of simple carelessness. There's also the perennial problem of bad backs. How many experienced cruising skippers have you met with degenerated disks and other such lumbar evils caused by careless anchoring techniques? I must confess I am among them, for years of energetic hauling in the wrong way have caught up with me. Here are some simple precautions to help avoid accidents:

- Insist that your foredeck hands wear gloves and deck shoes, even on a calm day.
- Tell everyone to keep his or her fingers clear of fairleads and cleats, especially when paying out an anchor line. If the line gets out of control, let go rather than hold on; otherwise your fingers will be crushed between line and fairlead. Accidents can be prevented by keeping a turn around a cleat or windlass gypsy.
- Always lift anchors and haul on lines using your legs rather than your back alone. If you have a bad back, let others do the work and follow the advice of your physician.
- Never allow a crew member to stand inside the bight of an anchor line (or any warp under strain, for that matter) or inside a loose coil of rope. There have been cases where crew members have been hurled overboard, entangled in a muddled anchor line that slipped suddenly when a stopper or cleat gave away. Snapping lines under strain can whip like snakes, breaking limbs in seconds.

Like so much else with anchoring, the simple routines of dropping and recovering an anchor have been surrounded with elaborate jargon, pseudo-science, and unnecessary mystique. Establish some simple routines that are effective for you, yet flexible enough for many circumstances. Then find a quiet bay and spend a day practicing your skills. You'll be amazed just how quickly the basics become second nature. And from there it's a matter of experience, of enjoying an art that never palls until the day you die.

CHAPTER FIVE

Anchoring Under Sail

"Give the poor anchor a chance!"

Donald Street, *The Ocean Sailing Yacht Vol. 11,* 1978.

THE ACTUAL TECHNIQUES and routines of anchoring under sail are unchanged from those employed when anchoring with the aid of an auxiliary engine. The operation becomes more complicated and difficult, however, because new factors come into play:

• You will have restricted ability to maneuver, since you do not have the fingertip control possible with an engine. However, it is amazing how easily you can sail backward, stem tidal streams, or heave-to within a restricted area if you must.

• Since you will not be able to place the yacht accurately, you should always have a convenient escape route or backup anchoring strategy in mind.

• Your crew will have to handle sails, sheets, and halyards as well as ground tackle.

• Once anchored, you will have much less ability to snub the anchor firmly by going astern

With practice, you should be able to minimize these limitations.

LETTING GO ANCHOR

When anchoring under sail, you have to maneuver the bow of the yacht to the exact place where you want the anchor to fall to the bottom. You cannot be going too fast or too slow. The anchor must also be near the waterline and rode ranged on deck before you approach, and the crew must drop anchor at precisely the right moment.

Two critical variables affect the way you should anchor under sail: wind direction and tidal streams or currents. When approaching an anchorage under sail, heave-to offshore or jill around until you have established the precise direction of the wind in the cove. Note the directions other yachts are swinging, and wind patterns on the water. Decide which approach course you will take, select several anchorage spots, and map out potential escape routes.

This is the moment at which you must decide how much sail to carry for the maneuvers that lie ahead. In addition to your normal anchoring preparations, place several more vital items on your checklist:

- Clear away your second anchor and range some chain and rode on deck so you can drop this anchor in a hurry. If nothing else, you can use it to check your boat speed.
- Stow sails that are not going to be used. Use several small sail areas rather than a huge genoa and main. Consider reefing the main and substituting a working jib for a genoa. (With a roller furler, reduce it to working jib size.) The small sails may be easier to handle in close quarters. Mizzens come into their own. Above all, have plenty of sail in reserve, ready for hoisting on short notice if needed. Roller-furling jibs are especially useful for anchoring under sail, because the furled sail is clear of the foredeck crew.
- Clear away halyard falls from their cleats, flaking the coils, so you can lower sail in a hurry.
- If you have a dinghy, have it ready for immediate use in case you want to lay a second anchor.

ANCHORING INTO THE WIND

This is the most common way of anchoring under sail, and is relatively simple if the wind and currents are in the same direction, or if current is negligible.

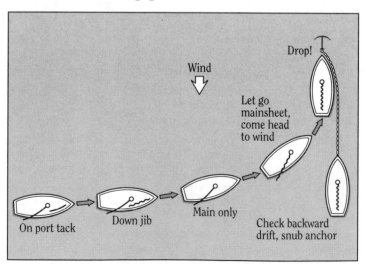

Coming to anchor against a headwind

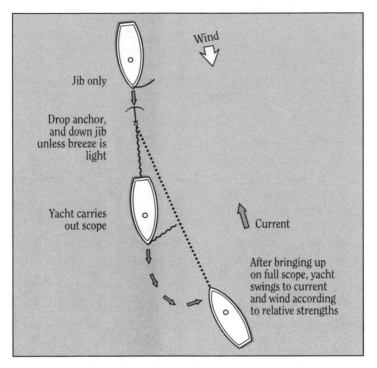

Coming to anchor under sail—wind against current, with current stronger.

Select the berth and approach it in a broad sweep, well to leeward. Some distance from the anchoring spot, lower the jib. The yacht slows. At the correct distance from the berth, round the boat up into the wind, leaving the mainsail flapping. Make sure there is no mainsheet tension, so the boat will not try to sail ahead. While one crew member stands by the halyard, the vessel comes to a stop in the correct place.

The crew drops anchor and pays out the cable smartly as the bow pays off downwind. Once enough cable is over the bow, the crew can check the yacht's swing and snub the anchor. When everything is secure and full scope is paid out, lower the mainsail.

What happens if the anchor drags or you foul up the approach? If there is space, you can pay off downwind, or by using a port or starboard tack, you can retrieve your anchor as you sail clear.

WIND AGAINST CURRENT OR TIDE

This is more complicated. Head into the strongest element—wind or tide. You can figure out which is stronger by observing other boats at anchor. Once you are clear, either run down to the anchorage, adjusting your sail area to slow your progress against the current, if it is the dominant factor, or beat up to your chosen berth if the wind is the stronger component. Remember that the favoring current will make you shoot a long way after you luff up.

In the former case, drop the anchor, paying out the cable until sufficient scope is laid. Then lower sail and check the boat. She'll usually stop across the current, beam to wind.

If you anchor in a tidal anchorage, be sure to check your cable when the tide turns and the yacht swings bow to wind and tide. At this point you should achieve a proper snub, if you didn't before. Be aware that the danger of dragging will be greatest when the tidal stream reaches its maximum strength, halfway between high and low water.

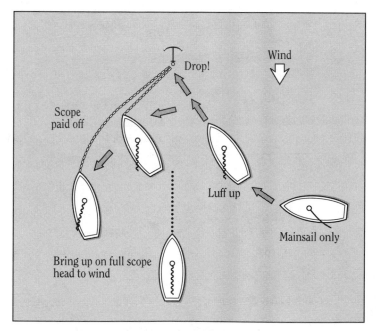

Anchoring with a beam wind

ANCHORING WITH A BEAM WIND

This situation typically arises in narrow, channel-like anchorages, where there is no space to beat. Approach your chosen spot on the lee side of the channel, easing your sheets to slow the boat. It's better to approach too slowly than too fast; you can always accelerate slightly. You should use the main for this maneuver, stowing the jib out of the way so you can anchor quickly. Have the anchor at the waterline ready for quick release.

Once to leeward of your anchoring spot, luff into the wind, letting go the anchor as you drift astern. Sheer the helm to one side or the other, so that the cable is carried clear of the anchor. If you are going too fast, you will overshoot the anchor and fall back over it, increasing the risk of dragging or fouling the lines.

As with all maneuvering under sail, the essence of the exercise is control of the yacht at slow speeds. Go too slowly rather than too fast.

ANCHORING WITH WIND ASTERN

Again, run down on your anchoring spot while controlling the speed of the boat with the jib, dropping the sail as you lower the anchor underfoot and then carry way until all scope is over the bow. With no tide or current to worry about, you can approach slightly faster than if against a stemming current. Finally, check the boat to ensure a good snub.

WEIGHING ANCHOR

Raising anchor can be trickier than dropping it, especially in congested anchorages. The problem is that you have to pay off on either port or starboard tack as the anchor leaves the bottom. The tack you choose depends on the direction in which open water lies. Unless you have boat speed almost at once, you'll run the risk of fouling your neighbors and drifting out of control. And, of course, the anchor must come off the bottom quickly.

Wind only, no current

Your boat is lying at anchor, head to wind, sheering only slightly as the breeze shifts in the gusts. Your neighbors will be well clear, provided you sail away on the starboard tack.

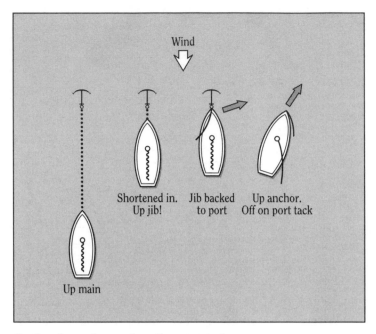

Getting the anchor under sail on port tack

First, hoist the mainsail, leaving the mainsheet completely slackened. If need be, you can use the main to sail up to the cable.

Second, pull in the anchor line to short scope.

Third, set the jib as quickly as possible. *A roller-furling genoa comes in handy here.*

Fourth, back the headsail to starboard, forcing the yacht onto the starboard tack, and break the anchor out of the ground. Then let draw, and sail away as the foredeck crew brings the anchor aboard quickly. If the anchor does not break out, let go the jib sheet and try getting the anchor out by hand, or try again with the backed headsail, waiting for a harder gust.

Wind Against Current

This is trickier because too much sail area will force the yacht over her anchor line on the bottom, since she may be lying stern to wind. Have both main and jib ready to hoist quickly, and a crew member manning the headsail halyard and sheet.

First, shorten your anchor line until the anchor is ready to break out

Second, set and sheet in the jib until it fills and the yacht begins to stem the stream.

Third, let the boat break out the anchor under sail.

Calm Conditions, with Current, or Very Congested Anchorages

Occasionally, you may be boxed in by other yachts, all lying to two anchors The wind may be calm, or there may not be enough room to pay off on either tack.

You can tow yourself out with the dinghy, but unless you have an outboard tender, this can be hard work. In a flat calm, with the vessel head to current, you can use your anchor as a brake, dragging it along the surface, while you steer the boat astern. If the wind is blowing through a congested spot and you cannot bear off, you can turn the boat end-for-end, set a headsail, and sail clear after retrieving your anchor over the stern.

Warping and Kedging Out

Few people warp out of anchorages these days, for much old-style seamanship has been forgotten since the advent of auxiliary engines. But the techniques are simple, provided you have good belaying points ashore, such as trees or bollards, and a sufficient supply of long ropes aboard.

Land two crew members with long warps. Have them belay as you heave in, moving ahead from shore point to shore point. Maneuver yourself into open water, where you can drop anchor again and make sail. Warping is an excellent method in narrow channels where you can run lines ashore, but it requires a couple of long heaving lines for success.

Whenever warping, you should control the warps with cockpit winches and the anchor windlass aboard. Never let the shore crew haul on your lines or take the full weight of the yacht. And always be prepared to drop an anchor at once in case things get out of control.

Clawing off a lee shore is when kedging comes into its own. As you start to haul up the main cable, send a crew member with the kedge in the dinghy out ahead at a slight angle. The kedge is then dropped from the dinghy, and the yacht lies to this as the bower is brought aboard. You then repeat the process as many times as necessary to get yourself clear. I would not recommend this procedure except in moderate conditions and with relatively light ground tackle, since the dinghy work involved is arduous at best.

CHAPTER SIX

Mooring

"Why lose sleep with one anchor, when you can lay two and enjoy a full eight hours?"

An Anonymous California sailor, 1992.

THERE WAS A TIME when you could anchor for days on end in places where there was plenty of room to swing. Nineteenth century cruising pioneers like the tough Claud Worth thought nothing of singlehanding 50-footers with their heavy Victorian gear and taking shelter with monstrous ground tackle in the lee of convenient English Channel headlands, however foul the motion. Today's congested anchorages have changed the rules. The wise skipper now cruises with kedge at hand. Many people view mooring—anchoring with two anchors—with fear and trepidation, when the process is really only slightly more complex than lying to a single anchor. This chapter examines some of the uses of a second anchor, and different ways of laying it.

WHEN TO USE A SECOND ANCHOR

Your kedge serves not only as an emergency anchor, substituting for the bower, but as a means of checking swing and minimizing the risk of dragging. The decision to lie to two anchors depends on a number of factors:

- Are there strong tidal streams or currents running through the anchorage that limit the deep water anchoring area? Typically, this situation arises in narrow channels with strong tidal streams. The Bimini roadstead in the Bahamas is a classic example. You must lie bow and stern to the current, so traffic can pass. The tide runs strong here, so you need heavy anchors at both ends of the boat. Even if the channel is uncongested, you have to be careful not to swing into the path of seaplanes landing in the harbor. As it is, they often taxi only a few yards from your stern.
- Is the anchorage too congested for everyone to swing to a single anchor? Some southern California island coves have

as many as 90 boats anchored in rows during summer long weekends.

- Is swinging room restricted? You may have a small anchorage to yourself, but there may not be enough room to swing without going aground. In this case, you'll need to swing around the anchor in your own length, or to lie in a single direction. Two anchors are essential for either arrangement. This is often the situation in the Pacific Northwest or Scandinavia, which abound in small gunk holes.
- Is there an uncomfortable surge in an otherwise safe anchorage? By laying a strategically placed kedge, you can face the yacht bow or stern to the waves and minimize discomfort. I have used a second anchor many times to ride bow-to the inevitable light swell that rides into California anchorages.
- Do weather conditions necessitate a second anchor? You may be lying in an anchorage where the wind changes direction abruptly during the night. A kedge laid out in the prevailing direction can reduce windage and add to your security. This is an important consideration in places where land breezes blow during the small hours.

LAYING OUT THE KEDGE

There are two methods of laying out your second anchor: either by dropping both anchors one after the other, or by using a dinghy. To lay out a kedge with your dinghy, first anchor in your chosen spot. Have the dinghy close astern, oars in place, ready for loading the kedge. (Some people prefer to load it ahead of time—it's a matter of preference.) With one or two crew members aboard, lower the kedge and chain into the stern of the dinghy so both can be thrown overboard without tangling.

One hand then rows while watching the skipper direct the dinghy course with hand signals. The other crew member pays out the anchor warp from the yacht, making sure adequate slack allows for free rowing. When the skipper signals, the dinghy stops and the stern hand passes out the chain and drops the kedge overboard, making sure it does not foul the line. Once the anchor has settled on the bottom, the crew aboard hauls in the slack, takes a strain on the rode, and maneuvers the yacht into the right position.

Before dropping a kedge from a dinghy, you should row beyond the spot where you want the anchor to lie. This allows for fall back as the anchor and chain sink to the bottom.

Once the kedge is on the bottom, adjust your scope fore and aft as desired.

For the purposes of description, we have assumed that you are laying out a kedge astern. Exactly the same principles apply with an anchor laid out at an angle to the bow. The most efficient way is to bring the stern of the dinghy under the anchor wherever it lies on deck, then have the crew row away and anchor in the right direction, while you bring the warp to the most convenient deck winch.

In days of yore, when anchors were much heavier, ground tackle was slung over the stern of a wooden dinghy. At the right spot, the lashing holding the anchor and chain in place was cut. This procedure saved wear and tear on the tender and is well worth adopting with your own wooden, metal, or fiberglass dinghy.

I strongly recommend that you use the dinghy method until you have gained considerable experience of anchoring in congested quarters. The possibilities for making a spectacular mistake multiply tenfold if you try and do everything from the boat herself. All it needs is one rode to snarl, or a signal from helm to bow to be misunderstood and a seemingly smooth maneuver can unravel fast.

Laying out a kedge underway requires fine judgment and a well-drilled crew. Begin by getting both anchors ready, ranging cable on deck at bow and stern. (Again, we assume you are anchoring fore and aft.) Station crew members at each anchor and approach your chosen berth. Reduce speed. Drop the kedge as you pass over the spot where you want the stern anchor. Pay out the line as you make way ahead, checking the cable momentarily to snub in the anchor. Then pay out more rode, using the engine to carry you to the spot where the bower goes overboard. (By this time, you will have double the final desired kedge scope.) Drop the bow anchor, go astern, and snub, hauling in the kedge line as you pay out the main cable. Once your bow anchor is snubbed, you can adjust scope fore and aft. Beware—don't get your kedge rode tangled with your propellor as you back down!

This maneuver leaves little room for error, but is deeply satisfying when you get it absolutely right—especially in front of a critical audience. One of the minor pleasures of cruising is watching other people anchor. It is amazing how the most

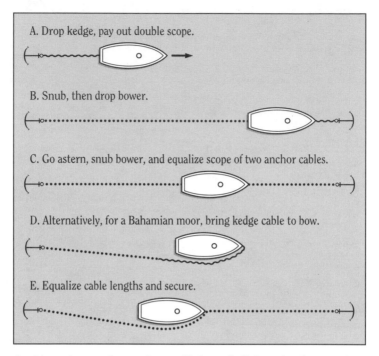

A. Drop kedge, pay out double scope.

B. Snub, then drop bower.

C. Go astern, snub bower, and equalize scope of two anchor cables.

D. Alternatively, for a Bahamian moor, bring kedge cable to bow.

E. Equalize cable lengths and secure.

Laying a stern anchor underway (A through C) is easier than putting the bow anchor out first. The Bahamian moor begins the same way (A and B), but the kedge line is then taken to the bow (D) before the rode lengths are equalized.

calm and rational people go berserk when the wind catches their stern, or their first attempt at anchor drags. All very entertaining to watch, until you remember that it could happen to you…why not row over and offer to help? You are most likely to run into problems as you drop the bow anchor and go astern. The kedge crew will have to use their line to prevent your boat's yawing out of control into other boats.

You can, of course, lay the bow anchor then back down, paying out double scope until you can drop the kedge over the stern. This offers less control than the method just described.

You can lay your kedge and bower under sail, but only with a beam or following wind. In either case, lay the kedge first, using your sail area and the anchor line for control until the bower is on the bottom.

OTHER MOORING METHODS

Mooring bow and stern is convenient when space is restricted and you are unable to swing. It works when everyone else is anchored "with the grain," in the same way, with wind and tide running parallel to the vessel, all with equal scope. If the wind or current turn at right angles to the yacht, however, the effect is that of a taut bow string, and you will almost certainly drag.

The so-called "Bahamian moor" allows you to swing in your own length. You lie to two anchors laid at 180 degrees to one another, with both anchor lines leading from the bow. The elegant way to lay a Bahamian moor is to drop one anchor astern, let out double scope to lay the other, and finally center the bow between the two lines to adjust your mooring spot. (I once watched Caribbean sailor Donald Street do this under sail, a classic exercise in consummate seamanship.) You can lay the second anchor with the dinghy, of course, but you will get a much better snub with the first method.

A Bahamian moor is superb in small anchorages where you want the security of two anchors in case of a sudden wind shift, but where swinging room is restricted. It is also very effective in tidal channels, where the ebbing and flooding streams come from opposite directions.

The "fork moor" uses two anchors at the bow, separated by an angle that can range from 30 to 120 degrees. An angle of 45 degrees is optimal in rough weather. This is a very useful moor in an uncongested anchorage in gale conditions, where you are weather-bound and do not want to drag. You can lay your kedge with the dinghy, or drop the bower first, motoring across to the kedge site as you pay out scope, then dropping back as you lay out rode to both anchors. When lying to two anchors in a fork moor, shifting wind and current may swing you around enough for the two rodes to cross in "a fouled hawse." If this happens, pass the inboard end of the more portable of the two cables around the other to clear them.

The fork moor is extremely effective when lying in a bay where the prevailing wind rarely varies and you expect storm conditions for some time. I have never had such a rig drag, even when anchored in 50 knots in a windy Spanish *ria* just south of Cape Finisterre.

Backing your bower with the kedge is a common technique in rough weather, and is described in Chapter 7, as is dropping an anchor underfoot.

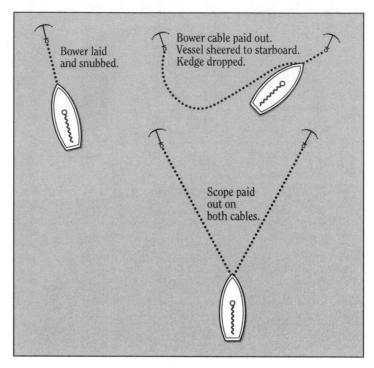

Bower laid and snubbed.

Bower cable paid out. Vessel sheered to starboard. Kedge dropped.

Scope paid out on both cables.

The fork moor.

RECOVERING TWO ANCHORS

To hoist anchor, you can either let out slack on the bow and recover the kedge from your stern, or lift the anchor from a dinghy. It can be a wet job with a dinghy, and should only be undertaken with a stable and well-designed tender. Always raise the anchor over the stern to avoid capsize. You are better off backing down, paying out scope on the bower, and picking up the kedge over the stern, using whatever winch is most convenient.

Recovering your kedge from a Bahamian or fork moor involves a similar procedure. In the case of the fork, motor and haul up to your kedge while slacking off the bower, making sure the slack line stays clear of your propeller. You can then swing to a single anchor while you get organized.

Mooring may mean more work, but it offers peace of mind. Once you have discovered how convenient and easy mooring can be, you will be surprised just how often you use your long-neglected kedge.

CHAPTER SEVEN

Heavy Weather Anchoring

"It was fine to see the line-of-battle ships pitching their great burly bows into the tumbling sea, the spray every now and then flying over their forecastles in a shower...They let go a second anchor, veered 140 fathoms of chain, and struck top-gallant masts at midnight."

Robert Edgar Hughes, Victorian yachtsman weather-bound in a gale-torn naval anchorage in the Baltic, 1855.

THE WIND SHRIEKS in the rigging in a never-ending, nerve-racking symphony. Sudden gusts raise the noise level, as the boat heels to the wind and sheers wildly, the anchor cable grinding in the bow roller. You lie on your bunk listening to the storm, wondering if you will stay put, waiting for the sudden swing that goes on and on instead of being checked at the bow. After even a few hours of a gale-torn anchorage, your nerves are on edge. You only relax when the wind drops and an incredible quiet settles over the boat. You drift off to sleep with a wonderful sense of relief—and a quiet satisfaction that you anchored right. Anchoring in heavy weather is a demanding test of the cruising skipper's seamanship.

Rough weather increases the windage on yachts and the strain on ground tackle. The basic routines of anchoring are the same, but there are things you can do to increase security at anchor. These include choosing a well-sheltered anchorage, increasing scope, lying to two anchors, and minimizing chafe.

While the foredeck crew ranges cable on deck, decide which part of the anchorage is most sheltered Consider not only swinging room and depth, but such phenomena as tidal streams, gust lines on the water, and headlands or buildings that may deflect the wind. Are there canyons which funnel gusts downslope into the heart of the anchorage? Can you lie out of the tide to avoid the confusing popple caused by wind against current? Is there enough room to swing to one anchor, or will you have to moor with two? Are yachts in the anchorage swinging wildly or dragging?

After making some preliminary decisions—one anchor or two, depth to lie in, general area that offers the best shelter, and so on—take a leisurely pass through the anchorage. Don't hurry. Take time to make careful decisions. As you make your pass, decide on approach lines, establish potential escape routes, and make sure your crew knows exactly where you will drop the anchor, and where you plan ultimately to lie.

As you approach, reduce speed to the point that you have sufficient steerage way to control the yacht in the gusts. You must keep her head to wind, avoiding uncontrolled sheers caused by gusts hitting the boat's topsides. Speed control is vital as you approach the anchor point. After you put the engine in neutral, it will be just seconds before the boat sheers away with the wind. The foredeck crew must let go the anchor at just the critical moment so that it lands in the correct place without losing distance to leeward. You can use the movement astern and sheer to lay the cable out along the bottom and to snub the anchor. Then pay out the scope, maintaining at all times a turn around a windlass or cleat. Be sure to run the engine hard astern for half a minute or so once you are at anchor.

In strong winds, raising anchor is more difficult than dropping it. Careful use of the engine is essential, with the skipper in the cockpit using throttle and helm to keep the boat to her cable. The trick is to keep the line slack so foredeck crew members can haul it in without breaking their backs. They should use hand signals to tell you which way the cable is lying, and whether to use power or not. Because the bow will swing in the wind, the crew must always keep a turn around a cleat or windlass gypsy to weather the strain of a gust without losing hard-won footage. Never allow the yacht to overrun the cable so it lies underfoot. You may damage the hull, and will have to wait until the boat rides back on the anchor.

Once the cable is vertical, the bow will snub and jerk in the waves. This may break the anchor out of the ground without warning, so you should be ready to apply power on signal from the crew. You will have little margin for error here, for if a gust breaks the anchor out, you will lose the strategic moments you normally have to abort raising the anchor when the anchor is at a short stay (directly below the bow). Also, as the line is shortened, the strain on the cable may be too great for the foredeck hands. Tell them to take a turn around a cleat. The chances are ten to one the boat will break the anchor out of the ground. Occasionally, you may have to pay out a little line to reduce shock loading. If the anchor does not break out, apply a short, sudden burst of power. This should do the trick without pinning the cable against the hull. As the boat pays off, the crew should haul in as fast as possible so the anchor can be secured in its fairlead before the boat hits rough water.

STAYING ANCHORED: SCOPE

Your ground tackle's effectiveness depends on ample scope. This is doubly true in rough weather. If the weather forecast predicts strong winds or an impending gale, go forward immediately and pay out more scope, using all you have if necessary. But before you do so, observe the positions of your neighbors. Is there ample swinging room for your increased scope? (Remember, letting out more cable increases your swinging circle.) In congested anchorages, you are better off moving than settling for cramped swinging room. Bear in mind the danger of other yachts with inadequate scope dragging into your boat. Remember, too, that in a congested anchorage, your extra scope may put you above a neighbor's anchor. What would happen if he or she has to raise anchor in a hurry in the middle of the night?

There may be times when your cable starts jerking and snubbing, and you will need even more scope on the bottom. This is when your extra warp comes in handy. By paying out another 150 feet or more, you ensure a more horizontal pull on the anchor which encourages it to dig in farther, as well as providing greater elasticity.

Flake your extra warp on the foredeck, then tie the bitter end to the base of the mast, a convenient cleat, or a samson post. Then unshackle or untie the end of the anchor cable from the chain locker and bring it on deck. If joining cable and warp, you are best off shackling the cable in a loop back on its own links, then securing the warp to it with a fisherman's bend or a bowline. Be sure to seize the free ends of any knots to the standing part, and to wire shackle keys tightly. Both knots and shackles can work loose as the cable slackens and tightens. Join two rodes with a bowline and fisherman's bend, or with two bowlines.

Once the lines are joined, you can pay out the knot over the bow during a lull, easing it over the bow fairlead with great care. The extra scope will serve you well, but remember to use line of adequate breaking strength. Knots reduce the strength of rope by up to 25 percent.

If the anchor starts jerking and snubbing, you can pass a bow-shaped anchor shackle down the cable, with 70 to 100 pounds of lead ballast or iron attached to it. The weight of the lead slides the shackle down the chain until it forms a catenary below the water. This reduces snubbing at once. When it comes time to hoist anchor, you can haul the weight back with a special line. Few people sail with anchor shackles and weights anymore, except for a few long-distance cruising yacht sailors. More's the pity, for shackles and weights work like a charm. I have not had much experience with them on anchor rodes (as opposed to chains), but suspect they would work well, provided you padded the anchor shackle bow with leather. You can also seize a couple of feet of the rode with marline and canvas, then use a premeasured length of line to slide out the shackle when you are at full scope. This ensures that the weight always rides on the chafe-proofed portion of the rode.

LYING TO TWO ANCHORS

You can use an additional anchor to gain greater security in rough weather. Well-proven methods include the fork moor, laying an anchor underfoot, and backing your bower or kedge line.

Fork moors were described in Chapter 6. However, in rough weather you should ease out more scope so the two anchors lie with an angle of less than 45 degrees between lines. This evens the load between both anchors and reduces the strain from a sideways pull. If you have both an all-chain and a nylon cable out, it is better to lie to the nylon. It has greater elasticity, and, should it drag, you'll fall back on the bower and chain.

Laying a fork moor can be difficult in rough conditions, especially if you have to use your dinghy to drop the kedge. If you do lay both anchors under power, be certain to tend your first line so it doesn't foul the propeller.

Many experienced cruising people prefer the security and ease of backing the anchor, or putting two anchors on one line. This provides tremendous holding power without the hassle of two cables. Backing your anchor is achieved by shackling your kedge with a 12-to 15-foot length of chain to the crown of the bower (be careful to wire the shackles). The backwards pull of the backing anchor holds the bower on the bottom and

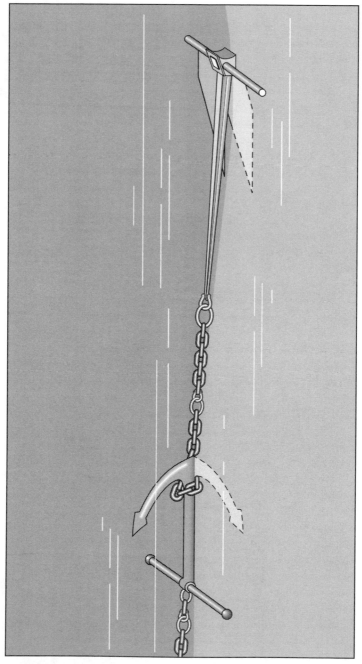

Backing your anchor

increases its holding power. The backing anchor can be as little as half the size of the bower, with the joining chain appropriate for the lighter anchor. Always keep a special length of chain available for backing. Some people use nylon line to join the anchors, but I think the weight of chain is preferable. It also reduces the risk of chafe.

When setting backed anchors, just drop them in the usual way, making sure they do not foul one another, and allowing the appropriate scope for bottom conditions and wind strength. Lifting backed anchors can be a devilish job. Some skippers use tripping lines to cockbill the backing anchor, but the best way is to grit your teeth and haul both to the stemhead.

If you want to add a second anchor to an existing single anchor on the bottom, you have no option but to reanchor, keeping the boat in position with the engine or a temporary kedge.

I would use backing only in extremely rough conditions, such as in winds over 45 knots. Under such circumstances, backing provides about the most secure anchoring there is.

SHEERING, CHAFE, AND RIDING SAILS

In rough weather, the windage of the rig can cause a yacht to sheer until it reaches an angle of 30 to 40 degrees off the wind. Once the anchor line checks her, she "tacks" over onto the other side. This can add up to very uncomfortable motion, with the boat heeling over in gusts and rolling from side to side as she sheers about at the end of her rode. The sheering also increases the severe strain on the anchor line by as much as a third in rough conditions. If you are anchored on poor holding ground or have to lie to a shorter scope than usual, the wild motion could break the anchor out of the ground.

Even in moderate breezes, the boat will sheer at anchor, grinding the chain or rode in the bow fairlead. You can chafe through a nylon warp in a few hours, even in a 15-knot wind. Make sure the edges of your bow fairlead are rounded and smooth, so that there is nothing to cut into the rope. Even if everything is as smooth as glass, swathe the rode in chafing gear at the fairlead. Plastic hose and old toweling serve well. Secure the gear tightly to the rode with lashings or sail ties, and replace it at once if there are any signs of wear.

You should inspect your rode at least every half hour.

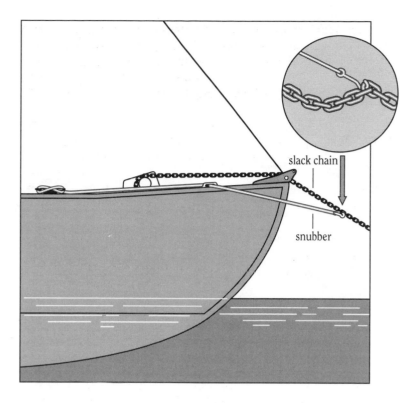

slack chain

snubber

Sometimes, the weather may be so rough that you cannot keep chafing gear in place. Under these circumstances, ease out the rode a few inches whenever the first signs of wear appear. This is sometimes called "freshening the nip," a trick often used by skippers a century ago on halyards as well as anchor rodes.

In extreme circumstances, you can reduce chafe and the chance of dragging by running the engine slow ahead during strong gusts.

Anchor chains are relatively immune to chafe, but are much more prone to snubbing and violent jerks. Some times the shocks on a chain can break out the anchor. You can reduce the load on the anchor in restricted waters or shallow depth by rigging as a shock absorber a 15- to 20 foot length of 5/16-inch nylon line. A chain hook at one end connects the shock absorber to the chain. You then thread the inboard end through a bow fairlead and attach it to a cleat, hauling in the chain slightly so that it droops in a bight between the chain hook and the fairlead. When a gust puts a load on the chain, the

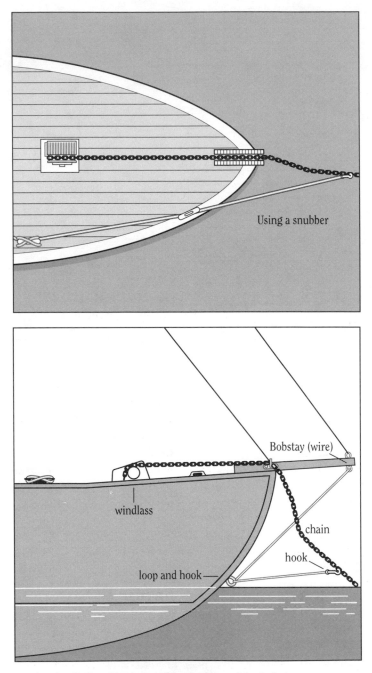

Using a snubber

windlass

Bobstay (wire)

chain

hook

loop and hook

Anchor bridle (snubber) rigged to the base of the bobstay

nylon stretches to the point where the chain again takes the strain. But the snubbing effect is cushioned by the expanding and contracting rope.

Some skippers end their all-chain cable with a long length of strong nylon line spliced to the chain. The nylon lies over the bow fairlead, letting the cable sink to the bottom. This arrangement works well, and has the advantage that it can be buoyed, and cut easily in an emergency.

Neither chafing gear nor shock absorbers will prevent even a fork-moored yacht from sheering, however. The best solution in that case is a small riding sail mounted on the backstay. Such a sail acts as a weather cock that keeps the bow into the wind: as the bow pays off in either direction, the sail brings it back. The ability of a riding sail to reduce sheer is truly astonishing, and its effect makes all the difference to your peace of mind.

Quite often, you'll see ketches or yawls lying at anchor with their mizzens set as riding sails. If you have a single-masted yacht, you can still rig a riding sail. Simply seize a small halyard block a suitable distance up the backstay, or use the main halyard to hoist the sail up over the stern. Leave the sail's foot lying to a long tack line so it is well clear of the deck. You then sheet in the clew to a convenient spot on deck, such as to the main traveler or to a pad eye. You can use your smallest storm jib for the purpose, but you are better off with a special sail. Many people cut down a used sail, but if you build a special riding sail, have it cut flat from very strong canvas so it can withstand long hours at anchor exposed to the hot sun. Use a sail area up to about 10 percent of your total working sail area, reducing that in extreme conditions when you may be overpowered by the 10 percent figure. You can fit reef points, enabling you to reef it in a hurry.

I once saw a cutter with full-length battens in her riding sail. The skipper told me that they reduced occasional slatting in strong winds.

ANCHOR BEARINGS AND WATCHES

Perhaps the worst things about anchoring in rough weather are the noise, the constant wind in the rigging, the heeling of the yacht as she leans to sudden gusts, and above all, the constant fear that the boat will drag. If the wind rises to gale force and you are in a congested or small anchorage, you will have to set anchor watches.

Shift by shift, 24 hours a day, crew members rotate anchor watch duty. A tour of two hours is enough, especially during the night hours. The watch keeper can shelter below, but should perform the following duties:

- Keep a constant watch on neighboring yachts and landmarks ashore to see if your boat is dragging. Come on deck for an all-around inspection at least every twenty minutes.
- Check the anchor line at the bow. especially for chafe, at least every half hour.
- Check all gear on deck, especially sails, making sure it is still securely fastened and not in danger of blowing away.
- Monitor weather forecasts on the radio. This is especially important in areas like the Pacific Northwest where weather systems move fast.

Despite an anchor watch, the skipper will probably lie half awake listening for the first signs of trouble. This is partly because responsibility lies in the captain's hands, but also because most skippers have another fear—that even experienced crew members will hesitate to call for help, for fear of making a fools of themselves over a possible false alarm.

Drum it into your crew members' heads: IF IN DOUBT CALL THE SKIPPER. Make sure they know you'll never be mad about false alarms, but really angry when they fail to call you. Once your crew has earned your trust, you'll sleep much better at night.

Anchor watches should be based on anchor bearings, or some other objective method of determining whether you are dragging. As soon as you come to anchor, take two or three careful bearings on conspicuous objects or landmarks ashore than can be identified at night. The crew member on watch can then check the bearings at regular intervals. If the bearings show signs of change, chances are the boat is dragging.

Sometimes good bearing spots are difficult to find. On occasion, I have lain to anchor with my Loran C switched on. So accurate is the reading that the anchor alarm would have sounded if I had dragged. A GPS can achieve the same effect, if the circle of accuracy is small enough. A depth finder with a variable alarm sometimes works over shelving bottoms. If your yacht is elaborately equipped, you may be able to use radar plots for anchor bearings. Some skippers install a remote instrument read-out at their bunk, so they can observe wind speed and direction, also the depth without getting up. Many navigation stations are similarly equipped, so someone sitting at the table has comprehensive data to hand.

No one enjoys lying to anchor in gale-force winds, but with sound ground tackle, ample scope, and careful forethought, you can minimize the trauma of one of cruising's inevitable experiences.

CHAPTER EIGHT

Some Anchoring Emergencies

> "When a Vessel comes to an Anchor...it is always prudent to take three Reefs in the Topsails before they are handed, as they will be ready, should a sudden Gale arise, if there is a necessity for running out to Sea."
>
> Darcy Lever, *The Young Officer's Sheet Anchor,*
> Philadelphia edition, 1819.

THIS CHAPTER ADDRESSES some of anchoring's sudden emergencies, most of which can be resolved by simple procedures that should become second nature.

DRAGGING ANCHOR

Dragging anchor is perhaps the most dreaded of all cruising emergencies, for it can happen on the calmest of days and at the most unexpected moments. If a sudden gust strikes the bow at over 45 knots, for example, the drag is dramatic and bone-jolting. The chain snatches, the yacht pays off downwind, and the anchor never checks the boat. The crew hears the jolting cable and, having had ample warning of the drag, tumbles on deck in a hurry.

"Silent" drags are much more dangerous. You may be sound asleep, and wake up the next morning yards from where you went to bed. Your only protection against silent drags beyond Loran and GPS is to anchor with extreme care, and with adequate scope. I learned this lesson the hard way in a quiet Caribbean bay, where we were tired and in a hurry to anchor before sundown. We anchored carelessly close off the beach in a flat calm. At 0200, I felt us heel and heard a soft grinding sound, for we had actually dragged ashore. It took us an hour-and-a-half of backbreaking work to get her off, a high price to pay for a careless piece of anchoring. Even on the calmest nights, the prudent skipper sleeps with one ear open, and occasionally looks out to check that familiar landmarks haven't moved.

Dragging can be caused by inadequate scope, strong winds or sluicing tides, by poor holding ground, or by using the wrong type of anchor for prevailing conditions. You can exercise some control over these causes, but not over the neighboring yacht that fouls your anchor line without your realizing it. Or there may be the coral head that breaks unexpectedly after days of holding you fast. Much dragging can be avoided by what one might call defensive anchoring—keeping clear of neighbors, selecting good holding ground, and using adequate scope and good snubs. But what should you do if you drag anyway?

Your first and immediate defense is to let out more scope. In most cases, doubling the amount of cable on the bottom will check the anchor and give it a chance to dig in anew. Once the scope is over the bow, go hard astern on the engine for at least thirty seconds to dig the anchor in again. For added security, consider a fork moor, or even hold the boat head to wind with the engine while you back the bower anchor with the kedge.

Such strategies work if you have room to maneuver and a margin of clear water astern. If, however, you have a rocky lee shore astern and the water is too rough to put the boat to sea, you will probably be forced to run your engine to keep undue strain off the cable. If there's a lull, try to lay a second anchor, either by motoring up to your bower, or by using the dinghy. But even after laying a second anchor, you should probably keep the engine running until the danger recedes.

ANCHORING IN EMERGENCIES

The time may come when your engine fails thirty yards from some rocks to leeward. Your sails could be torn, the wind may be blowing in your teeth. What do you do next? You anchor—in a hurry. Time and time again, your anchor can save you from grounding and other mishaps. Follow the golden rule: ALWAYS have your anchor ready for release in a few seconds when maneuvering near land. Anchors check your way, hold you off shallows, and give you time to pause and think your way out of trouble.

In many cases, such as when your propeller is fouled by a lobster pot line, or a plastic bag blocks your water intake, you may be tempted to flee from the danger as quickly as possible. But in most cases, unless the weather is bad, you are better off anchoring just to give yourself time to think and get organized. Lay out a scope of three to five times the water's depth. If the anchor holds, start the engine to ease the strain on the cable while you fix the problem aboard. If the engine has failed, flake out all the scope aboard, prepare your dinghy, and lay out a second anchor as well. If you have to sail clear of a lee shore and doubt whether you can sail out with the anchors, abandon them. Attach buoys, or even spare life jackets to the bitter ends, then cast off. You can return to pick up your anchors and cables later.

FOULED ANCHOR

In these days of congested anchorages and mooring filled estuaries, the chances of fouling your anchor are higher than ever. Normally, the first sign of a fouled anchor is its resolute refusal to break out of the bottom. It may be jammed under a rock, lying under a mooring cable, or caught in a neighbor's chain.

You may be able to clear the foul by lifting the anchor with the trip line, if it is buoyed. A second alternative is to use diving equipment. With good visibility, a scuba-certified crew member should be able to identify the problem and possibly correct it on the bottom. In clear water, you may be able to work out a way of clearing the foul by snorkeling over the anchor. Some yachts carry a sighting box that substitutes for goggles, or even an emergency diving cylinder.

Much depends upon whether the chain or the anchor itself is fouled. You may find, for example, that the anchor is caught on a coral obstruction. In this case, you can sometimes winch short and let the sawing action of the boat dislodge the anchor in a few minutes. More often, the muddle requires more sophisticated maneuvering. I once had my rode wind itself around a coral head several times. The only way to untangle it was by intricate maneuvering using the dinghy and a snorkel mask.

An alternative and often highly effective method, especially with Bruces, Danforths, Deltas, and CQRs, is to run a weighted bight (loop) of rope down the cable onto the anchor shank. You then slacken the anchor line and wrench the anchor clear of the obstruction using the bight. You can sometimes free a cable trapped under the anchor line of a later arrival by hooking a grapnel under the offending rope or chain and lifting it clear. A weighted bight of rope is often more effective, because you can slide it along the cable. The grapnel method is rarely effective, except in clear water where you can see what you are doing.

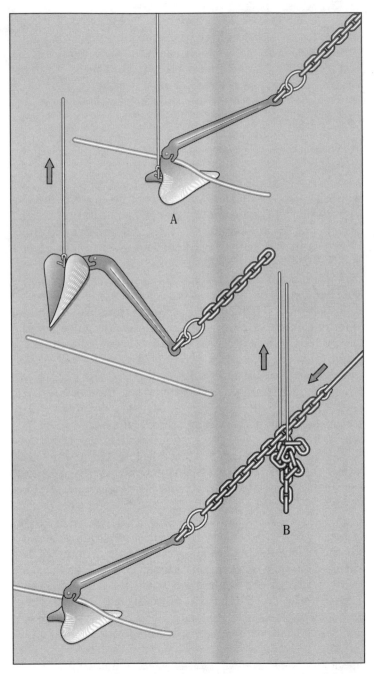

Clearing fouled anchors with a trip line (A) or a bight of rope (B).

A couple of times, I have been able to clear a foul by winching the mess to the surface, then clearing up the tangle from a dinghy.

None of these methods is fail-safe. Your best protection is to minimize the chances of such hazards ahead of time. Do so by avoiding commercial anchorages and mooring areas, as well as rock or coral-infested coves. It's a good idea to carry a sharp knife, both for cutting kelp from your anchor, and also for freeing anchor lines entangled around your propeller.

GROUNDING

Those rare occasions when you go aground may be the moments when you really appreciate what your anchors can do. In shallow water, where stirred-up sand can block engine water intakes and where sails may blow you even farther onto the mud, anchors are a reliable and effective weapon, even in rough conditions. A combination of well-placed anchors and powerful winches can work miracles.

The circumstances of grounding vary infinitely, from a minor beaching at the side of a narrow tidal channel to a full-blooded stranding on a coral reef. Unless you are off in a few seconds, always lay an anchor into deeper water, if for no other reason than to prevent the boat's going farther aground.

Once efforts to ease yourself into deeper water with sails or engine fail, you should lay out your anchor in water as deep as possible, using as much scope as you can. Using the dinghy, lay out the anchor at an optimum angle from either bow or stern, depending upon where the deepest water lies. With windlass or sheet winch, haul in the anchor line until the compelling strain eases the boat into deeper water. Sometimes you may lay the anchor at such an angle as to allow you to pivot the boat toward the deepest water. The first sign of movement will be a turn, followed by a gradually accelerating forward motion until the boat lies at anchor rather than aground. You can then heave short and raise anchor at your leisure.

In tidal waters, you will probably find the rising tide will float the boat off ground, provided you take the precaution of laying an anchor in deeper water. If you don't lay an anchor, the chances are you'll drift even farther aground.

At other times, you may run the boat onto the mud at full speed. The yacht will be hard aground, and attempts to haul her into deeper water may fail. To get her off, you must reduce draft by heeling her to port or starboard. One ingenious method involves flooding your wood or fiberglass dinghy and suspending it from the end of the boom. However, you will be better off laying out an anchor far abeam, leading one or more halyards to the rode from the masthead, and taking up the slack by heaving on the line from the deck. You can then careen the boat by leading the line through a block on deck and heaving it with a strong winch. Once the keel lies less deeply in the mud, the yacht should slide off into deeper water, especially if you use the bower to assist in the process. This technique works well, but requires considerable muscle power and powerful winches—to say nothing of numerous young muscles!

Extreme strandings on coral reefs or river bars lie outside the scope of this book. There may be rare times, however, when the boat drags anchor and drifts ashore onto a reef or sand bar, leaving the yacht lying on her side in shallow water close to the anchorage. You may be able to haul her off by careening the hull with an anchor connected to the masthead and using two more anchors lying to bow and stern to ease the boat into deeper water.

LEAVING ANCHORAGES IN A HURRY

Over and over, disaster strikes crowded yacht anchorages when gales roar in without notice and turn fair-weather coves into wave-ravaged lee shores. Comfortable and well fed, with warm bunks beckoning, skippers relax their vigilance and ignore not only official forecasts, but telltale weather signs as well. The wind and swell rise in minutes, coming too quickly to allow for a safe getaway. Boats are trapped on a dangerous lee shore. At best, skippers and crews will face danger during some tension-filled hours. At worst, boats will drag ashore, possibly with loss of life.

Only one rule applies when rough weather is combined with even a slightly marginal anchorage: *Put to sea if weather conditions deteriorate.*

Knowing when to get out and when to stay anchored requires careful judgment that often stems from bitter experience. You should certainly get out when

- Weather forecasts call for rapidly deteriorating conditions and strong winds that will blow into, or cause rough seas to surge into, your anchorage.

• Local weather conditions such as veil clouds or slow swells in still water presage severe conditions.

• The wind starts blowing onshore, or swell conditions make the anchorage uneasy.

• The anchorage becomes too congested for safe anchoring in strong winds. It's safer to move from such a situation *before* an emergency arises.

These are guidelines. You have to make your own judgments on the spot, considering the general weather forecasts with both local weather conditions and the nature of the anchorage you are using. To move or not to move is a matter of vigilance and constant sensible judgment. As a general rule, you are much better off getting out early, or even unnecessarily, rather than hanging on until disaster is imminent.

If you must make a rapid getaway, or face the possibility of one, you are better off lying to one anchor than two. A second anchor reduces your maneuverability, and you run the risk of tangling the rode around the propeller if the line runs astern. Prepare by making sails ready for hoisting, warming up the engine, and briefing the crew. Get the dinghy aboard and stow the yacht for sea. Be prepared to leave on a moment's notice.

Most often, you'll have enough warning to leave with some leisure. But if a real emergency hits, you may have to slip your cable. Have a large anchor buoy handy, clearly labeled with the yacht's name. Attach this to the nylon pennant at the end of your anchor line, and be sure to throw the slipped line well clear of the bow. Drift clear so the propeller can turn freely. When the weather improves, you can return to pick up your anchor.

There are some conditions under which no anchor will hold you in place. It is to avoid possible disaster in such situations that you slip your cable and wait out the bad weather at sea. In fact, you'll be far more comfortable there than lying sleepless off a raging lee shore.

CHAPTER NINE

The Mediterranean Moor and Other Techniques

"Ships are moored with an open Hawse to that Quarter from whence the most violent wind is to be expected: and it is of the greatest consequence to keep the hawse clear..."

Darcy Lever, *The Young Officer's Sheet Anchor*,
Philadelphia edition, 1819.

T HIS CHAPTER COVERS a miscellany of thoughts not only about anchoring itself, but about small details of lying at anchor.

MEDITERRANEAN MOORS

The so-called "Mediterranean moor" is used mostly in French and European waters. With it, yachts are anchored off a quay, then backed in, with warps securing the stern to convenient bollards a few feet offshore.

Mediterranean moors involve intricate maneuvering in close quarters, so preparations should be made well ahead of time. Lower and stow your sails, removing the hanks of any jibs on the foredeck. Prepare your bower and cable for anchoring, rig fenders on either side, and flake down two long warps attached to cleats on either quarter. Have your dinghy in the water, with a crew member ready to row ashore with warps when the time comes.

While the crew prepares the deck, take a careful look at your potential berth. Check the wind direction and place the yacht head-to-wind, upwind of your chosen spot, at a slight angle to windward of the gap in the row of yachts. Allow ample distance to lay plenty of scope. Check the lay of your neighbors' anchor lines At the same time, spot key bollards and rings on the dock ashore.

When everything is ready and the yacht is in the right spot, drop your bower, go smartly astern, and get a secure snub well clear of other yachts. Then send a crew member off in the dinghy to lie close on the quarter prepared to take the windward mooring line.

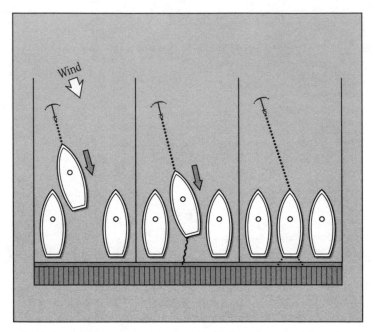

The Mediterranean moor. First, lay the anchor to windward, snub in, and back down. Back into the space and take the windward line ashore. Adjust position after taking leeward stern line ashore.

Back down slowly, with the bow crew member paying out the line around the windlass or cleat in a way that enables you to check way in seconds. Use your rudder to back between your neighbors. When close enough to the shore, send the dinghy ashore with the windward line or throw it to someone on the quay. He or she should secure it to a bollard or ring so you can winch yourself toward shore from the yacht.

When the windward line is ashore, you can maneuver the boat in foot-by-foot until the stern is the correct distance from the dock. Meanwhile, the leeward stern rope goes ashore and fenders are adjusted. You can adjust your position by hauling in stern warps and anchor line as needed.

In very congested situations, you may have to lie between the bows of two larger yachts, leading your warps onto their foredecks. This kind of berth is insecure at best, and advisable only in calm conditions.

RAFTING UP

Sometimes you may feel sociable and want to raft up alongside a neighbor. This is fine, provided the weather is calm and there

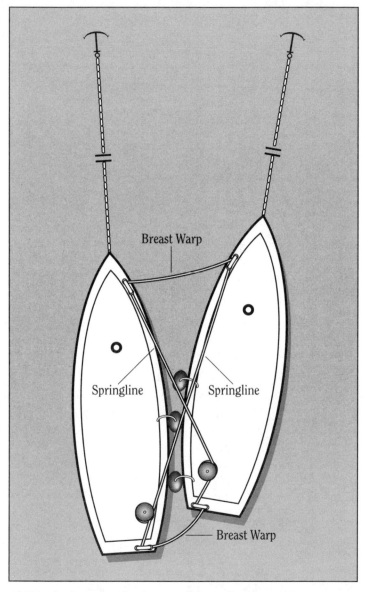

Rafting up. Note that the springs are taut, the masts of the two yachts are staggered, and the breast lines are relatively slack.

is negligible surge in the anchorage. But be sure you can cast off quickly if the wind or surge increase. It is very easy to smash lifelines, topsides, and even masts as two yachts grind together.

The two yachts should be anchored at a safe distance from one another, then their anchor lines should be slackened off and the boats should be secured together. Two taut spring lines led to the jib winches will hold the boats tightly, while the breast warps at bow and stern should be left relatively slack. Plenty of fenders are essential, while the masts must be staggered to prevent rigging tangles and costly damage.

Never raft up in anything but calm conditions, and avoid doing so on one anchor. You will swing too much.

DEEPWATER ANCHORING

In these days of congested anchorages, you may often have to anchor in water much deeper than the optimum 25 to 30 feet.

At first glance, depths of 70 feet or more may seem intimidating. But in practice they are no trickier than shallower anchorages, provided you lay out ample scope. In a depth of 80 feet, with three times the soundings in chain over the bow as scope, a considerable deadweight rests on the bottom. This will keep your boat in place even under stormy conditions. If you expand that scope to five times water depth, you will be in even better shape.

If you plan to anchor regularly in deep water, carry an all-chain cable. You will bless the extra weight, and the yacht will veer around much less at anchor. However, with all that weight over the bow, you will have to be very fit and strong to haul the cable aboard. Invest in a powerful manual or power windlass. Be sure that your hawsepipe and chain locker are self-stowing, so you don't have to spend valuable time feeding the cable below decks. Mark your cable at 50-foot or 100-foot intervals. This enables you to monitor the amount of scope going over the bow.

When dropping anchor, place the bow of the boat in a position that allows some sternway before the anchor hits the bottom. It takes some seconds for the ground tackle to pass through 70 feet of water, so you should judge your anchoring position accordingly. You may find it difficult to judge the quality of your snub. Run the engine astern for at least 30 seconds once you think you have a good snub. Place a hand on the cable to "feel" the anchor on the bottom.

If you anchor in deeper water most of the time, increase the weight of your anchor to as much as 60 pounds for a 40-foot boat. The extra weight will do no harm, and your anchor winch will handle the work involved.

COPING WITH TIDE

In many places, such as the Virgin Islands, California, or the Mediterranean, the tides are too negligible to be of consequence when anchoring. But the time may come when you anchor in a tidal cove where anchoring at the right depth may mean the difference between comfort and a rude awakening.

In tidal waters, you should always have tide tables and atlas at hand. Everywhere you go you will need to know the day's tidal range, particularly during those days of the month when spring tides are running. Your choice of anchorage may be affected, too. For instance, a French cove may offer ideal shelter, good landing, and smooth water, but sailing directions tell you that the ebb tide rushes through the bay at 6 knots, leaving dangerous whirlpools and a rocky bottom in its wake. Clearly, you should anchor elsewhere.

When selecting a tidal anchorage, you need to know whether there is ample water at low tide. The appearance of the anchorage when you arrive may be deceiving. What may seem like a large cove when you enter at half tide may be a tiny creek two hours later. To lie safely, you need ample swinging room for your scope at low water. Check the charts to be sure you will have sufficient water and won't swing into shoal water.

Inevitably, the changing water depth will alter your scope. You could have a nasty shock if you veer 45 feet of chain for a low water depth of 15 feet in a 30-foot tidal range. At high water, you'll be drifting! Always veer the right amount of scope for rough conditions at high water, not low. If swinging room is restricted, you might want to adjust your scope as the tide rises and falls.

In tidal anchorages where the directions of ebb and flow are in opposite directions, you must be careful to dig in your anchor hard to prevent it from breaking loose at the tide change. One solution is a Bahamian moor, which enables the yacht to lie with the tide (see Chapter 6)

DRYING OUT AT LOW WATER

There is something mildly intimidating about deliberately laying your boat aground. People sometimes lay their yachts alongside a post or a quay at high water, so they can scrub and paint the hull between tides. In extreme circumstances, they beach their vessels to avoid letting the boat founder from a catastrophic leak, or after a collision. Few skippers have ever dried out to find shelter in a tidal anchorage where deep water is congested or unavailable. They are deterred for several reasons—fear of grounding, lack of special equipment, or sometimes a reluctance to try something new.

Most people have the idea of a grounded yacht lying at 45 degrees on a mud flat, while the crew crouches uncomfortably on the angled deck. There's some truth in the image, for only a handful of yachts lie upright on the mud. Multihulls, twin-bilge keel yachts, and some with flat bottoms and lifting keels are comfortable drying out. Many working boats, such as the celebrated Thames barges with their leeboards, were specially designed to spend much of their lives on tidal flats.

Conventional monohull yachts, particularly those with full-length keels, need special "legs" to hold them upright while drying out. These consist of hinged wooden or metal timbers with feet that are secured to the rail of the yacht on either beam and held with fore-and-aft lines. When the vessel is to dry out, the crew lowers the legs, which are the same length as the boat's draft. The boat then settles comfortably upright in a sheltered anchorage.

Anyone sailing seriously in tidal waters should fit legs. They are a cheap method of expanding your cruising range into uncongested waters. For the benefit of those who want to fit legs here are some pointers on drying out:

When planning to dry out, you should look for places where the tidal range is at least equal to the draft of the yacht. The bottom should be entirely uncovered at low water. Your berth should be well sheltered at high water so there is no risk of pounding as you settle on the bottom or float off.

Sand, gravel, or shingles make the best bottoms for drying out. They offer a firm surface for your boat's legs, and for your legs, if you have a ladder aboard and want to walk ashore. (Return before high tide, however, or you may have a long wait!) Mud can be treacherous, especially when one leg sinks in deeper than the other. Look for places where the bottom is horizontal, both fore and aft as well as laterally, and avoid underwater obstructions that could either damage your keel or damage or dislodge your boat's legs.

Before deciding to dry out, consult your tide tables and check that the tides are "making," that is to say, the range is increasing the next day, not decreasing. Otherwise you stand a chance of being "neaped" and having to wait two weeks or so before there is sufficient water on which to sail away. You can, of course, use the tide tables to calculate the exact moment you will ground. This is useful when you are grounding to clean the bottom between tides.

Even when drying out, be sure to lay adequate scope to hold your boat in rough weather at high tide.

LYING AT ANCHOR

Nothing is worse than rolling uncontrollably at anchor. Rolling results from swells hooking around headlands into anchorages, or from minor night winds setting up aggravating popples in the dawn hours. While you can work miracles using a kedge to set your boat head-to-swell, you may also want to invest in some "flopper-stoppers." These take several forms, among the most elaborate being a rectangular frame filled with plastic baffles. You lower this from the end of your boom or spinnaker pole, set at right angles to the yacht and secured fore-and-aft from the end, with the "flopper-stopper" under the water surface. People who have used these frames report excellent results, although I have achieved comfort with a weighted plastic bucket.

Finally, how many times has your beauty sleep been disturbed by your fiberglass or wooden dinghy bumping gently against the stern? Old hands used to sink a bucket at the dinghy's bow to keep it well astern. This works quite well, but I favor tying the dinghy alongside against a fender, or tying the dinghy with the end of her painter connected to the end of the spinnaker pole or boom, which is swung out at right angles to either side. To recover the tender, you simply swing the pole or boom inboard.

In these and many other minor ways, you can make life at anchor so pleasant that I wager you'll prefer lying to your trusty ground tackle to being crowded sheep-like in an expensive marina. Standards of seamanship have declined, the purists cry! Maybe they have, but you can help restore them by enjoying to the full the noble art of anchoring—or, if you prefer a more earthy term, staying put!